D1155446

Dear
Joe;

May, 05

Embracing Life

I hope you
find hope, wisdom
& inspiration,
along with some
humor!

Warm Regards,

Lois

Embracing Life

Living With Chronic Pain

Lois V. Pike

iUniverse, Inc.
New York Lincoln Shanghai

Embracing Life
Living With Chronic Pain

Copyright © 2005 by Lois V. Pike

All rights reserved. No part of this book may be used or reproduced by any means, graphic, electronic, or mechanical, including photocopying, recording, taping or by any information storage retrieval system without the written permission of the publisher except in the case of brief quotations embodied in critical articles and reviews.

iUniverse books may be ordered through booksellers or by contacting:

iUniverse
2021 Pine Lake Road, Suite 100
Lincoln, NE 68512
www.iuniverse.com
1-800-Authors (1-800-288-4677)

ISBN: 0-595-34705-3

Printed in the United States of America

This book is dedicated to my husband, Wilbur L. Pike III, whose unconditional love and support have been an enormous help to me during the past eight years; also to my deceased parents, Helene M. Vogt, who encouraged my love of poetry as a young girl and to Albertus D. Vogt Jr., who made me read "Scientific American" magazine instead of comic books, thus teaching me how to solve problems thinking outside the box.

Acknowledgements

Writing this book has at some times been a very healing and inspirational process for me and at other times a long and tedious one, but always inspired by love.

I wish to thank my brother, Albertus D. Vogt III, for showing me how to overcome some of life's most difficult situations and for allowing me to share in his life and teaching me about brotherly and sisterly love.

Special thanks to John Scherer and Lynnea Brinkerhoff; whose Leadership Development Intensive workshop changed my life forever.

To my daughter Alayne and her husband Brian Washburn, whose constant love and support have helped me through some very rough times, along with my grandsons, Ethan and Graham who eloquently express their love for me through their gifts of music, soccer and track.

To my daughter Amy and my beautiful granddaughters, Kendra and Olivia, who never fail to call me almost every day, and for providing me with their unique gifts of laughter, amusement and basketball games.

To my special Stepdaughter, Cory Pike, for her constant love and support, along with providing me the latest and greatest pharmaceutical information available.

To Michael Spiegel, MD, of Arthritis Associates of CT & NY for his utmost professional care and guidance (Dr. Spiegel was recently voted by his peers as one of the Top Ten Doctors in the State of Connecticut) and to his wonderful nurse, Nancy Brutz, who has what it takes to get the job done.

To Aparna Oltikar, MD, one of the best family physicians on the entire Planet Earth, for her devotion to her patients, and to her assistants, Robin Dean and Lori Coty.

To Diane Bray, APRN, who has skillfully guided me through this journey, thus enabling me to choose the best paths for the future.

To God from whom all blessings come, for His inspiration and undying love for me, His child.

Introduction

This story begins on a cold winter morning in New York City on December 30, 1943, where I was born the 3ʳᵈ child to Helene Russo Vogt and Albertus D. Vogt, Jr. My oldest brother passed away 2 days after birth and my only existing sibling is my brother Albertus D. Vogt III (Bert), born November 2, 1939.

The first 10 years of my life still remain a blur to me, as you will see in the contents of this book and life for me really began in south Florida, where the family returned to after many years. Daddy was born and raised on a plantation in Dunnellon FL and Vogt Springs was named for his family. My grandfather was the discoverer of phosphate and began mining in the 1800's. He also fought as a teenager in the Civil War and there are numerous articles and much history concerning our family.

Bert's interests lay in music, horticulture and cooking. My interests swung in the direction of athletics, sports, singing, dancing and writing poetry. While unconditional love was not the order of the day, one had to perform in order to be recognized. This was evident to me as a very small child; thus I assumed the role of scholar student, athlete, etc. I had to be perfect and nothing less was acceptable.

I graduated in the top 10% of my class and paid my way through the beginning of college. Since schoolwork always came easily and I scored exceptionally high on my college entrance exams, I was stunned to discover that I had not developed any study skills whatsoever, and never finished the second semester.

I had been working part-time since the age of 15, so I simply went to work. The harder the task, the better the challenge. I married quite young and had 2 daughters during the first 4 years of marriage. I had difficult pregnancies and worse deliveries. Childbearing was not my calling either. So back to work I went. Raises, promotions, and awards were a constant source of validation for me as they always proved that "hard work pays off in the end".

At the age of 26, my body started to revolt, developing uterine and ovarian tumors, which resulted in a complete hysterectomy. The Doctors immediately put me on massive doses of estrogen, which resulted in benign breast tumors, which subsequently had to be removed. Did I really have time for this? Absolutely NOT. So I informed the Doctors to give the medication to the next lady in line, as I had to go about living my life.

Shortly thereafter, I developed severe Osteoporosis and Osteoarthritis, and within a 5-year period, I fractured my right shoulder, left elbow, tailbone and left hand (in separate incidents). Now I ask you, wouldn't any intelligent woman pay some attention to these matters? No, the answer for me was to simply work harder and ignore my body and soul.

Needless to say, the marriage bore the brunt of my hard driven personality and after several separations; we finally divorced shortly after our 29th anniversary.

By this time, the girls were out on their own and I decided to throw myself into my career with even more enthusiasm! For someone so smart, I certainly turned out to be a slow learner. I simply buried the past and forged ahead full throttle. My work was always centered in commercial banking and I enjoyed working at large insurance companies, attorney offices and finally the banking industry itself. I always hired, trained, promoted, rewarded and kept the best hard-working staff in existence and they became the family I did not have any longer.

While attending a 3-day seminar dealing with stress management, I found myself intrigued by the professor, who was himself ending his 27-year marriage. I was the class brat and challenged everything he put in front of me. He found the way my brain worked to be quite "interesting". After a few months of e-mailing our differences, we began to date. We are happily married partners who appreciate compromise, stress, and devotion and will have celebrated our 8th anniversary as this book is completed.

The girls (Alayne and Amy) eventually married and we are currently blessed with.4 wonderful grandchildren (Kendra and Olivia & Ethan and Graham). After pushing myself way passed my bodily limits, my body simply broke down. I spent an entire summer going through tests for Lyme Disease, Bone Cancer, etc. and was finally diagnosed with an acute flare-up of Fibromyalgia. At first the pain was so overwhelming that I was afraid I was actually going to die and then it intensified and I prayed that I would die. That set me back for a complete summer, but did I slow down? Nope, just forge ahead and you'll be fine I told myself. My husband was now beside me and beside himself trying to get me to slow down, but I would not hear of it.

I was blessed during the next summer with the opportunity to attend a 4-day seminar along with my husband Wilbur, entitled: "Leadership Development Intensive" put on by John Sherer and Lynn Brinkerhoff. We did many imaginative things and did some deep relaxation and memory trailing along with daily Yoga.

This seminar changed my life! I began to retrieve some very ugly memories from early childhood and vowed then and there to resolve some important issues.

God let me continue on my own free will until I developed uncontrollable diarrhea. I lost 30 pounds in a few short months and while standing directly in front of my boss, a Sr. Vice President, I had another attack. OK God, you win. You now have my undivided attention. My body was an empty tank with no reserves and my 5'5" frame had dwindled down to 108 pounds. I did not have an eating disorder, I simply couldn't absorb or properly digest my food. I was put on complete bed-rest and another battery of tests was ordered.

Now I had to be quiet, still and rest. Since I never learned how to do that, I knew I was in for some real trouble. I spent the entire fall and winter in bed, doing nothing except dealing with chronic pain. Additionally, the Fibromyalgia flared its ugly head again and I was doomed. What am I ever going to do about work now? The answer was simply NOTHING. I was put on disability (I still do not like that word or what it implies) I prefer the label of "Limited Ability". Well Lois, I said, your body may be shot, but you still have your mind so let's get to work and heal yourself, I devoured every self-help book I could find, continued to fuel my body with food, counseled with several doctors and finally understood that I must address the past before I could move forward.

This writing began in the very small Town of Litchfield in the Northwest corner of Connecticut, where we are fortunate enough to live in a country farmhouse, which was built in 1820. Needless to say, there are constant projects to be done and the house has been completely renovated, sticking with the times around 1820. The book thus began in the dark of winter, through the beautiful spring, into the summer, which we never really had, then into the spectacular fall and then a return to winter again. I continue to write these poems, as they tell the story of embracing life with chronic pain and hopefully from a patient's point of view, these words are meant to encourage all those who suffer with pain to continue to look inside yourselves and not be afraid of what you might find.

Some readers may wish to use this book as a daily journal, entering their own thoughts after reading mine.

I continue to be blessed with healing of body, mind and spirit, but that continues to be hard work. I have left the banking to those next in line. I finally want to live life to the fullest and gracefully accept all the love and blessings God has to share.

Happy Reading

January 1st

It is New Year's Day—last year is over
A time to begin anew, a chance to recover
From the pain of the past—a new time to live
A time to heal—another chance to forgive

Last evening was wonderful—a time to celebrate
Among other things, my 60th birthday
With good friends, good food and plenty of dancing
A time to renew our love—a time for romancing

The New Year is here and I am thankful for rest
For I really did push by body to the test
I truly want to be just like the others
With plenty of life out there yet to discover

And so I am happy with friends to love
They are sent to me from the angels above
My husband, my friend, and yes my lover
Sleeps with me peacefully under the covers

January 2nd

The pain and stiffness I am feeling today
Came as no surprise—the price that I pay
For pushing too hard and trying to keep pace
With the rest of the world running the race

Why is it I feel that I must keep trying
Not to accept my weakness and keep on denying
The truth of the matter is that I feel less
Of a person because I have this illness

I've been home from work over two months now
And I think no one remembers my name or how
I rebuilt the department that was quite a mess
And turned it around into a working success

The work is still there—I know from the calls
Of the few people who care and are not afraid of the falls
That result from my not being there to guide
Which leaves many exposed with no place to hide

January 3rd

It's the weekend again and I'm still at home
While I sit here and attempt to write in poem
How disjointed I feel from the world at large
And realize that I am no longer in charge

The pain and the spasms just seem to get worse
I'm supposed to feel better—instead I feel cursed
Fibromyalgia and Osteoporosis are enough to bear
But now this gastro problem has me in total despair

There are blood tests and cat-scans yet to endure
And more tests to come of which I'm not sure
I'm trying to keep a smile on my face
It feels awkward, strange and so out of place

I know the doctors are doing their best
To find the real problem using test after test
I feel like giving up and quitting the fight
I know in my heart I'm not a quitter—that's right!

January 4th

The Colonoscopy is scheduled for tomorrow at 1:00
And the preparation and process I want to run from
But I follow the directions right to the measure
And in the end I am sicker than ever

My body is dehydrated to the point where I lie
And hope to God that I really might die
I've never been sicker before in my life
And wish I could cut out the pain with a knife

Wilbur is beside me and beside himself too
He is watching and hates not knowing what to do
The night is endless I'm unable to sleep
I lay awake crying and softly I weep

There is not much more of this I can endure
I feel so forsaken by God I am sure
That He has abandoned me—left me alone
And then I remember "Footprints" carved in stone

January 5th

The day that I dread is finally here
We drive to the hospital and I am in fear
The nurse has difficulty finding a vein
Which does nothing to ease my frustration and pain

They finally wheel me into the room
The technicians seem cheerful but I feel like doom
The sedative is injected, but it does not take
And I go through the procedure totally awake

I am filled with rage, pain and disgust
These are the people in whom I placed my trust
It is finally over and no one can believe
That the meds did not take—so they come to see

I want to go home and forget this day
To sleep off the pain and curse all the way
Where are you God—why aren't I dead
He whispers to me there is still work ahead

January 6th

If work is ahead I don't want to play
Forgive me God—I can't even pray
Is this is the way You treat those who are blest
Please leave me alone—I just want to rest

I know I don't listen to You very well
And to get my attention, sometimes You must yell
I'm resting now and am ready to listen
What is it You're telling me that I'm not getting?

Dear child of mine did you think this was easy?
To speak to you when you're so carefree and breezy
It is then that I realize how I take life for granted
He has given me a lesson—a new seed to be planted

I'm beginning to see a new path for my life
He's asking me to share my story of strife
It's about embracing life living with chronic pain
To have courage each day to get up and try again

January 7th

Today I awake with gastro-intestinal pain
I barely can make it to the bathroom again
I have not yet had anything to eat
And this comes as yet another defeat

Food is passing through me in less than one hour
It is trip after trip to the bathroom and I holler
This just has to stop I can't take any more
And then I pass out cold on the bathroom floor

We phone the doctor to see what to do next
She suggest the BRAT diet and plenty of rest
I'm too weak to argue—so it's to bed I go
My whole body is throbbing and I've never felt so low

I remember to pray but can't finish my appeal
Sleep comes gratefully—perhaps God will heal
Please help my husband to deal with this mess
For he too is tired and in need of his rest

January 8th

My body is shaken with so much trauma
It seems like a soap opera filled with drama
I'm losing too much weight, which I can not afford
And now I'm afraid to eat—please help me Lord

I'm still so unclear what You're asking of me
I want to respond but I can't seem to see
I think You are telling me to put myself first
That seems so un-natural—won't I be cursed?

I think I remember the words of my mother
Take care of yourself before you can help another
I've let everything come before me for so very long
Work and troubles that to me do not really belong

How is it I've missed this message so clearly
That I've forgotten to treat myself gently and dearly?
The lesson I'm learning is so hard to take
It is that I am worthy, which is not a mistake!

January 9th

Today it is off to the doctor we go
My weight and blood pressure are far too low
She again prescribes more rest to heal
This body that needs so much it's unreal

The stress has built up and I have ignored
All the signs that clearly have been laid at my door
I'm truly amazed that I shut off my brain
Until with full force my body was in pain

There are good days between but not strung together
And so I must find my own way to feel better
The doctor is there to suggest and prescribe
But in the end—the choice is mine

To follow the path that is set out for me
Or to ignore it and never again be pain free
It is so hard to stay home and not go to work
But I know in my heart which plan will work

January 10th

It is Trivia night and I am anxious to go
For I missed the last game due to feeling so low
I promise dessert—so it's lemon cake I bake
It is such a hit there is little home to take

The game is fun but we're one couple shy
Donna has had surgery, chemo and I don't know why
My illness seems small in light of the news
She is doing very well, but without her we lose

We play in teams—women vs. the men
The score over time is even but then
We all realize that we know our favorite topics
And laugh in the end—we are stuck in the tropics

Good friends and good food are truly a joy
And we are all blessed to know and enjoy
The company of each other and what that really means
For without love and laughter, life doesn't mean a hill of beans

January 11th

Today is a Sunday—a day of complete rest
I feel like I'm really being put to the test
Wilbur is out cutting wood to fuel the fire
While I lay around simply feeling tired

I truly am trying to get rest and to sleep
But how much longer can this program I keep?
I feel like I'm not making a fair contribution
To the household and all that's involved in its function

Wilbur gives me assurances me day after day
There is nothing for me to do and nothing to pay
He really does have things under control
But I am having trouble accepting my new role

I'm reminded each day how much I am loved
When neighbors show up like angels from above
With food in hand which they know I will eat
And help me to get back up on my feet

January 12th

It is Monday—a new week has begun
But the day ends in horror and we are all stunned
Frank Jr. has suffered a heart attack and is dead
He was only 42 and many tears are being shed

Annie just buried her husband last year
And a daughter Diane in her teenage years
And now she must bury another child
Life seems so unfair—the whole thing is wild

But her faith sustains her along with friends
I am again amazed at how tragic life ends
Frank left a wife and three young sons
Who must pick up the pieces of life and move on

I am humbled again at how I complain
About my illness and all of the pain
But God is here in the midst of us all
To answer our prayers if only we will call

January 13th

Today is Tuesday and I cannot attend aerobics
For I have no reserves and too many limits
But the day moves along quietly and then it is time
For evening supper, some TV and then to recline

I took a few phone calls from some folks at the bank
With all kinds of nosy questions about this and that
I felt like I was being questioned and interrogated
To see if I was returning and was my job already taken

I'm truly not trying to think too much about work
But still I feel guilty and sometimes like a jerk
I know it's not my fault I got sick and had to leave
But I do still feel that I am responsible, this I believe

To get the work done and be a leader to my team
Is totally ridiculous if you know what I mean
It's not that I'm great or that I feel proud
It's knowing how little control there is over the crowd

And so I talk to Wilbur and he tells me to be still
To listen to music and to get a sense of God's will
I am only one human, not in charge of the world
Please tell me again God, I need to hear Your word

January 14th

It's the middle of the week, the day Wilbur loves
It's Wolleyball in the court with friends and then they go
For pizza and some brews at their favorite hang-out
A time for them all to have fun and talk about

Anything that is on their minds at the time
They all ask for me and that makes me feel fine
They are Wilbur's good friends but over time
I realize that they have also become mine

How lovely to know friends no matter the gender
We can express our true feelings, loving and tender
Or the surprise at how the world looks at things
Like bias and race and the stuff that life brings

I'll go to bed early, after soaking in the tub
Wilbur tries not to wake me as he climbs into bed
He touches me softly and I know I'm safe from harm
As I lay sweetly in the harbor of his arms

January 15th

It is snowing again, when will this ever stop?
Living in the northwest corner takes quite a lot
Of stamina, heartiness, strength and gut
The very things I am lacking and so I stay put

Safe in the house, with the woodstove to warm me
And make me feel toasty, like cookies and tea
That sounds to me like a very good idea
I'll make some as soon as I'm finished here

I put the kettle on to brew some good tea
The kind I know is beneficial to me
I'm making every effort no matter how small
To learn to live life and let the chips fall

The tea is soothing to my body and brain
It lets me relax and to shut down the strain
Of living with pain while trying to embrace life
Thank you God for my parents and my life!

January 16th

We were scheduled to see the dentist today
But the roads are too icy to pass, hooray
The dentist is not my favorite place to be sure
So it's back to the warm toasty bed I am lured

The day lingers on like most of the others
With nothing special to do and nothing to bother
Wilbur works from home today, making a plan
For a presentation tomorrow for some special clan

I'm weary myself in body and soul
And need some movement to clear the dull
The housekeeper is scheduled, but I phone her today
And ask her if she could please wait until Monday

She says that is fine as she has a lot to do
I know in my heart this has got to be true
She has three kids herself and then her mother
She helps her to deal with the loss of her brother

Thank you dear Lord for another day
A time to do nothing and a time to pray
I know that You know I'm doing the best that I can
Please don't ask for too much more, just hold my hand

January 17th

Today is the day of my mother's passing
It's been fourteen years to the day
I speak to her often as much as I can
I hope she is aware of exactly where I am

I call my brother and we both remember
Her very slow passing from a rare bone cancer
She was a great fighter and a good inspiration
And only left this world when we gave her permission

We promised to take good care of each other
Like and good little sister and brother
We are still very close—we phone quite often
Just to keep up and to speak with each other

The day does bring sad memories to mind
The arrangements to be made and the Mass to plan
We chose very carefully which songs would be sung
And we did it all beautifully with God's help along

People filled the church and were quite amazed
That our music group sang—the church was ablaze
Fr. Frank and Fr. Lou celebrated the Mass
And lifted our mother so high off the glass

She lives in heaven now with Daddy and no pain
For on this earth, her life was a huge strain
She did not do much in the way of complaint
But her eyes told the message of torture and pain

I'm glad she is free from the bonds of the earth
And somehow I just know she can see
The pain and the suffering of her daughter and son
And wished she was here to heal everyone.

January 18th

Today is a Sunday—a day to reflect
On the trials and blessings of the past week
There have been many of both to bear
I hold on to them—they're my life to share

I sent Kendra some money for Basketball Camp
I know just how much she wants to attend
But her parents have just bought a house and then
Things start to break and there's no money again

There is much excitement around the new house
And well there should be, it is beautiful
But big sister has yet to stop by or to say
Anything about it, approval or nay

This seems so unclear to me, I don't understand
The dynamics and competition between my girls
Is something totally beyond my comprehension
I don't play a part, but still I feel caught in the tension

January 19th

A new week begins and I'm feeling a little better
It is cold in the house so I don a big sweater
Wilbur starts a fire in the wood stove
And I begin to relax and it's no longer cold

The day is uneventful, and that is wonderful
I've had too many days that turn out quite painful
I start some laundry to keep myself busy
And try to feel useful and not to go crazy

I'm really looking forward to those warmer days
When I can relax outside—perhaps in the chaise
Then will come time for planting and weeding
Relaxing in the swing and catch up on reading

I've just learned that Granny is looking to move
She is excited and happy—a look that I love
She is a dear lady and at 90 years old and she
Has more wits about her then some folks I know

The place she has chosen is near Mary Jane
Which will make her life easier and less of a strain
She thinks it such an adventure and I am amazed
To think about moving would leave me quite crazed

January 20th

I'm gifted again with another new day
But this one is not as easy to say
There is a lot of pain of which I'm tired of dealing
I would gladly give up and trade for some healing

I rest and rest and then rest some more
I want to get moving and head out the door
To just go for a walk and breathe some fresh air
But it's too cold and icy and I know not to dare

I must learn to have more patience—that is for sure
But the lesson is difficult—I want so much more
My life lacks purpose and laughter and drive
I wonder when and if it will ever arrive

I must be more positive in my outlook
I'm reading some very encouraging books
But translating the words to life is so hard
It's like learning new tricks with an old deck of cards

January 21st

The middle of the week and I've not done much
The pain is still with me—I'm sensitive to touch
I wear my pain patches to take off the edge
And end up too tired and back in bed

The pain lessens but does not go away
Could I please have just one good day?
A day just for me to do as I please
With hours to play like a child with ease

My outings have been to the doctor and then
To the hospital, pharmacy and back home again
With an occasional trip to the lab to draw blood
I feel like a rosebush with thorns and no bud

This info is needed to uncover the cause
But I need a break and time to pause
To reflect on myself and the real outcome
With God's help they'll know where the pain is from

January 22nd

It is Thursday and the day for my visit
To Doug for a haircut to pick up my spirit
He jokes with me making me laugh out loud
And I feel better already as he does his job

He is so very kind and good to me
I so much enjoy his great company
He asks if I'm going out to a dance
He knows very well that there isn't a chance

But he tries very hard to make me feel merry
And I joke along with him like a princess fairy
I tell him that I must get some new shoes
So that I can dance and be beautiful too

He knows by looking into my eyes
That my laughter is really pain in disguise
But we each go along pretending all the way
And when I get home I remember to pray

For people like him are not easy to find
He makes me forget and I leave the pain behind
At least for an hour I'm free to be me
Thank God for you Doug and thank God for me

January 23rd

I've been blessed with time to rest and reflect
But time lingers on and I'm not better yet

I am able to look at the future and see
That better times are ahead for me

My body is weak, tired and small
I want to feel healthy, strong and tall

The hardened snow lies on the ground
And the trees are barren all around

I'm waiting to hear the music of spring
When the birds return and are happy to sing

The sweet songs and melodies that I love
And are clearly blessings from heaven above

Like having your faithful love for a guide
We face forward together—side by side

January 24th

It is sunny, bright and cold today
I do not mind, we get to see Kendra play

Her favorite game—the one she loves best
Basketball rates above all the rest

As point guard she brings the ball up the floor
And occasionally she even shoots to score

The jersey she wears is number 52
I call her the "bomber"—she shrugs and asks who?

Her face is set as she runs the pace
A look Wilbur calls "the Grammy face"

I love her so much my heart does swell
And she writes with words of love that tell

Of her love for me, a love deep and strong
It began long ago—before she was born

Pain and stiffness are there for me to bear
But they are lessened and I do not care

I get to see the smile that I love
Which is truly God's gift from heaven above

January 25th

Today is a Sunday with special time to pray
A day for both learning and some time for play
A visit to church—53 miles to the door
To receive special blessings and learn even more

The voices of angels sing sweetly from above
We visit my brother—the musician we love
We meet and greet friends we've not seen for awhile
With our arms open wide for embraces and smiles

The service is over—we bid our farewell
For it's off to Granny's to sit for a spell
Granny is 90 and loves when we visit
We like to go often and try not to miss it

But we forgot to make time for us alone
And I am very sick when we finally arrive home
The lesson of pain is to learn how to plan
The things that I can't do vs. the things that I can

Stretching the limits of each new day
Often lead to discouragement and to dismay
There must be a balance—this seems like a test
To adjust the right timing between doing and rest

The lesson is hard—time for me and then pain
But tomorrow will come and I get to try again!

January 26th

Today I am resting for most of the day
God calls to me softly, reminding me to pray

My body is healing—but I want to live large
He reminds me gently who is really in charge

I've been given this time to help ease the strain
Of yesterday's busyness, havoc and pain

When will I learn with patience in tow
To know and to trust just how far I can go?

It seems that I push the envelope too far
And I want to improve and keep raising the bar

The pain is lessened by sleep and by rest
But I continue to want to be known as the best

I am humbled by pain and resist with all my might
To do nothing today—somehow I know this is right

This disease that I have keeps me on my toes
It strikes out of nowhere and nobody knows

So yes, I will listen to music, rest and pray
God has graced me with yet another good day!

January 27th

My heart is peaceful, my body in great pain today
Disappointment looms large—this is not the day I planned
There is snow in the forecast, the sky is so gray

White cotton candy will soon fall from the skies
A new blanket of snow will cover the ground
I marvel at the beauty with great wonder in my eyes

A sprinkling of stardust to give us all hope
And a major distraction for those folks at work
While God covers the earth with a brand new coat

A reminder for each of us to breathe in life slow
But we are all in a hurry with no place to go
A time to show kindness to both friend and foe

I relax now and understand why I am here
To slow down the pace—I have hurried far too long
God whispers to me there is nothing to fear

And still I struggle to get the message clear!

January 28th

It is snowing so softly—God covers the earth
With a new dress of white—a sign of rebirth
There are many beautiful things if I look
But I open the pages and do not read the book

Like the "Arc of Light" which renders mirth
And is God's promise to the people of earth
There are rainbows around but I fail to see
The new life ahead that could set me free

I am anxious and quite a bit fearful today
A new doctor to see—more tests on the way
My pain is familiar—it sits by my side
And sometimes I wear it like a martyr with pride

Pain is awful to bear, but it does have its uses
It allows me to refuse without making excuses
I've tried to make a connection with diet and weather
Hopefully this new doctor can piece it all together

It is difficult at best and I am afraid
But I want to feel better and so I must be brave

January 29th

The day began both gloomy and glum
But by mid-afternoon out came the sun

It was off to the health store to purchase good buys
Recommended by the doctor who is indeed very wise

She implied that my body was an empty tank
Without the reserves on which I can bank

I must fuel this body to gain strength and relieve
The pain, which impairs my progress to achieve

It is a daunting task that lies ahead
To follow the path and then rest in bed

I must pay attention to everything that I do
With the help of God I begin life anew

January 30th

Today started off as it ended last night
With both of us angry and too tired to fight
Our misunderstanding was all about facts
Which left me upset and unable to relax

The day improved much as we left for school
To have lunch with Kendra—that really was cool
She introduced us around to teachers and friends
Who all had great things to say about her in the end

She was happy to take us to the school's book fair
Her favorite place is to read in her chair
She devours up books one after another
And reminds me so much of my librarian mother

We left to come home—I was able to rest
Before preparing dinner for our very special guest
Joey arrived with his usual good cheer
With presents in hand for us he holds dear

Our dinner was wonderful—his company a delight
I truly am blessed—pain left for the night!

January 31st

It is time for this pain in my body to leave
So I'm following the plan in which I believe

The doctor says I must put on some weight
And reclaim my life before it's too late

I arose fairly early the day to begin
And fight this pain with a great effort to win

We went to Kendra's game, I shouted so loud
She made some great plays and I am so proud

She runs the floor—it seems like a mile
And my pain is subsided—at least for a while

We come home, have dinner and watch some TV
Today I feel fortunate just to be me

I'm off to bed to rest my wear soul
And count the day's blessings—a million in all

February 1st

It's Super Bowl Sunday and for the very first time
I don't really care about which teams are on the line
I'm sidelined myself like an injured player
Spending most of my time in resting and prayer

This disease that I have will be with me for life
But I'm learning new ways to deal with pain and strife
I've been led to the doctors whose knowledge and care
Are helping me to live life and to overcome despair

I'm so grateful to have a day with some fun
I feel like a child who's been set free to run
Wilbur is my supporter, my cheerleader and fan
He encourages me daily to do the best that I can

I'm lucky to have him as husband and friend
Together we fight this great pain to its end
As each day winds down I remember to say
Thank you and thank God for my blessings today

February 2nd

I awoke today in much pain again
So I spent most of the day in bed
A reminder that although progress is being made
There is still a long road ahead

I want the healing to move swiftly along
I am tired of having to rest
And then I'm reminded whose timetable we're on
It is God, not me who knows best

I drink my rice water and have soup to calm down
And even relax in the bath
It took many years of stress in my life
To get to this place—and I laugh

How silly of me to think I'm in charge
That I can rule my body at will
It has its own mind and tells me again
To be quiet, go slowly and be still

February 3rd

Today is much better—I sleep in late
I have many things to get done
I busy myself with checkbook and paper
The mail arrives and here is the fun

A valentine card from my two favorite girls
My granddaughters, Kendra and Olivia
Enclosed is a picture they made just for me
One looks silly, the other looks sillier

I track all the medical bills for the year
When I finish I am totally stunned
The cost is enough to send one to college
I am shaken by love and am humbled

But no matter I have no regrets and I press on
For I'm loved and cared for by many
God has been gracious and kind to me
I could not ask for more—not one penny

February 4th

I was restless and edgy for most of the night
I went up to the loft very quietly to write
I'm amazed at how much pain is still stored inside
I crack the book open, but am afraid to open it too wide

There are memories from childhood filled with disgust
But the people involved have long ago turned to dust
I', aware that I should pray for my enemies too
If I'm truly to be healed, this is what I must do

The memories linger—I try not to dwell
And wish with my heart that all were really well
I am growing and learning at such a fast pace
It is hard to be still and listen with grace

I know that the future holds good things in store
But I am impatient and want to know more
The process is like traveling to another land
But God holds me safely in the palm of His hand

February 5th

It is off to the doctor this morning we go
To check on my progress which is going too slow
Yesterday was filled with intestinal distress
There is now great concern, which we must put to rest

It seems as if the gastro problem has a life of its own
With food passing through me in the fast-lane zone
We must tackle this problem—it is now too great
I can not afford to lose any more weight

I gain 3 or 4 pounds and believe this is a good start
And then the problem appears and we're back in the dark
This is lunacy because the tests reveal nothing
And yet here I am—112 pounds and still struggling

I'm eating good food and sometimes it stays with me
And then there are days when it travels right through me
Needless to say I have little or no reserves
And this is both taxing on my body and nerves

We had a great dinner and watched the UCONN game
The girls playing the best, beating the Tennessee team
I hope Kendra watched it because after school days
She'll be off to camp at UCONN to learn all the plays

February 6th

It is snowing, sleeting and nasty outside
I sleep in again and when I arise
Wilbur has done two loads of laundry
He is busy at work in his office and calls to me

"hey Cutie" he calls and I can't help but think
What have you had this morning to drink?
He just wants to greet me with hello and good morning
He knows I've had good sleep because I am yawning

Amy phones to tell me that she's home from work
She sounds like a foghorn and I ask if she is hurt
She has called the doctor and gotten some meds
I tell her she sounds like she should be in bed

Kendra is home because of the weather
This is a good thing—she can take care of her mother
Olivia is at daycare—a good place for her to be
It allows Amy some quiet time to sit and have tea

The day goes by slowly, I'm in pain again
But I'm certain the weather is playing its game but then
I'm sitting in front of the computer to catch up
On the events of the day and the feelings in my gut

Basically, all around, I'm feeling a bit better
And if Long Term gets approved with a check and a letter
We should be all right, but it worries me still
It's another form of stress I could do without well

February 7th

Today is Saturday and I get up fairly early
Wilbur is surprised; he is happy to see my so girly
I offer to make breakfast and he is delighted
For that means I must have slept through the night

I make us some omelets, which are quite divine
He gobbles his up before I make mine
I ask if he tasted it—he says it was "yumful"
He's happy to see me eating and feeling so useful

Since Wilbur is usually in charge of the kitchen
A job he truly loves, and also not to mention
It allows him to be very creative and free
Making meals that he knows very well will please me

He is the cooker and I am the baker
The roles we chose when we first got together
Our lives are quite different than most other couples
We talk and concur on most things in double

My life is improving with Wilbur by my side
We wish we saw more of our children from both sides
His lovely daughter Cory who lives in the west
And his son Andrew, whom we seldom see at best

It is so hard to know when to push or pull back
When basic communication is missing or lack
But things will work out I am sure before death
That God has a plan for us if we only have faith!

February 8th

It is Sunday again, a good time to rest
I use my time wisely, I think for the best
I catch up on phone calls and write my rhymes
Then turn on the TV, it's Basketball time

The day passes on with no trouble spots
I've had time to read and learn quite a lot
I'm attempting to learn a bit more every day
By reading and resting and taking time to pray

Wilbur is in his workshop I think making gifts
He knows that I love handmade things; oh what a lift
To think that his love for me is so deep
He'll spend time in the shop, week after week

The day winds down and I head off to bed
I'm tired with all the articles that I've read
I listen to music that lulls me to sleep
Wilbur holds me snugly; I'm his for keeps

February 9th

It is Sunday again, a good time to rest
I use my time wisely I think for the best
I catch up on phone calls and write my rhymes
Then turn on the TV—it is Basketball time

The day passes on with no trouble spots
I've had time to read and learn quite a lot
I'm attempting to learn a bit more every day
By reading and resting and taking time to pray

Wilbur is in his woodshop, I think making gifts
He knows I love handmade things—oh what a lift
To think that his love for me is so strong and deep
He'll spend time in the shop, week after week

The day winds down and I head off to bed
I'm tired with all the articles that I've read
I listen to music that lulls me to sleep
Wilbur holds me snugly; I'm his for keeps

February 10th

The day begins better; that would not take much
I did not get enough sleep so I'm not really in touch
With my feelings except that I'm tired and in pain
I'm feeling remorse about my efforts in vain

My work has defined me for far way too long
I am more than my work, I am very strong
I must shake this feeling of failure and defeat
And replace it with hope, I must set a retreat

This writing has helped me to get through each day
And I do remember to take time to pray
I know in my heart there's a reason to be
Which God has not yet chosen to reveal to me

I'll be seeing the doctor again tomorrow
I hate to look this pained and in sorrow
Progress needs to be made and peace of some kind
Along with my body, my soul and my mind

Things are still unclear as to what lies ahead
I want to know which part of the past I must shed
It is time to move forward, of this I am sure
And so ends the day with hope for the future!

February 11th

It's off to Dr. Spiegel we head
I'd rather stay here in my cozy bed
I know he is going to be disappointed
Because I'm not feeling well and am so disjointed

My weight has now dropped to one hundred eleven
Which is totally unreal and unacceptable
He asks if I'm eating and we both tell him yes
How to stop this fast moving train is anybody's guess

He tells me to head down the hall to the lab
To draw some more blood which will help him add
A new indication of what is the matter
I think to myself who cares and why bother

For what's happening to me is leaving me weak
Too tired to argue what I really need is sleep
We agree to meet again in six weeks time
We head home again this time feeling not too fine

But tomorrow will come and with it new hope
That I'll be feeling much better and less like a dope
What we really need here is someone in control
God are you listening it's me again calling

February 12th

It's haircut day again and so I get ready
To go out for a while I'm feeling quite steady
It's always great fun to visit the shop
I know everyone there and they always stop

To say hello and ask how I'm doing
Which is such a delight to watch everyone moving
Around each customer they make such a fuss
It amuses me because that's why customers trust

I certainly know that Doug would never take
Less time with me because he wants to make
Me feel beautiful at least for a while
And I always leave with a kiss and a smile

This day is no different except that I'm tired
A short outing leaves me weak and mired
But I must continue my venture outing
To do some interesting valentine shopping

I get home before Wilbur arrives
And my stash in a good place I find to hide
Now I am really in need of some rest
So it's up to the loft I go for the test

To see how long I can stay awake
Not very long for sleep to take
Hold of my body and thankfully get
The rest that I need I'm happy you bet

February 13th

I have had broken sleep throughout the night
And so I am grouchy and pick a fight
I blame it on Wilbur because of his snoring
Life without Wilbur would indeed be too boring

When I get up I realize there is great pain in my joints
I can barely walk and it scares me to the point
Where we call the doctor to ask what to do next
The pain medication I'm taking has no real affect

She phones in a new script to the pharmacy
Wilbur picks it up and gives it to me
It takes the edge off and I start to itch
I must be allergic—I think life is a bitch

But then we discover that antihistamine
Will stop the itch and let me sleep off the pain
It is then that I look at the calendar and see
That it's Friday the 13th—how strange can that be

I go back to bed and get up for dinner
This is one hell of a day—surely not a winner
In my book I need a day without pain
Oh please hurry spring and bring your fresh rain

February 14th

Today is the 14th; it's Valentines Day
A day for lovers—thank heaven I say
For Wilbur is without a doubt the very best
Husband and friend to that I will attest

I get up early his presents to find
He does the same he is so gentle and kind
He opens his first on that I insist
He's pleased with his presents and gives me a kiss

I open a mysterious carved box with something inside
A new watch and bracelet in just the right size
I make us both breakfast—it's really brunch
He is so happy to see me he's pleased as punch

The day goes by swiftly I'm feeling a bit better
I send him off to go visit his mother
I'm not up for the ride and so I stay home
I think about all the love and blessings as I roam

Through the newspaper I am struck with awe and wonder
There are love notes to read and I pause and ponder
The words are so easy to say once a year
I am so grateful I smile with a tear

For I am fortunate to have a partner
Who tells me each day how his life is happier
For each of us knows how bitter life can be
But with each other life is a wide-open sea

February 15th

Today is Sunday; a day of true rest
I do not put my strength to the test
I read the paper and then take a nap
Thank God for the freedom to do just that

Wilbur is working on programs for the week
I go up to his office for a kiss on the cheek
He is tired of working; he takes a break
For coffee and bread that's just been baked

Together we do make quite a good team
We realize we have a good life like a dream
It has its troubles but we take them in stride
We are honest with our feelings there is nothing to hide

We both know that there will be changes ahead
Especially for Wilbur who is adjusting in his head
For he will no longer be able to work on his own
He must find a job away from our home

It causes me great pain to know this is fact
For I no longer can work with this body intact
My main job now is to rest and recover
I feel so useless but the choice is no other

Wilbur has told me that for the past few years
I have carried the burden of money and tears
And now it is his turn to work for some other
Who will pay him the value of what he can offer

We need both the money and good benefits
My medical bills are killing us besides the scripts
We pay our co-pay and then besides that
We must pay for the coverage the entire fee in flat

It is dismal to think he must take a job outside
To obtain the benefits such a job will provide
But that is the way we agree to go
We are happy for love and what the future will show

February 16th

Today is Monday and Amy phones me
From work with an offer that pleases me
Kendra has asked to come visit her Grammy
She wants to remain close to her family

I ask her which days she has in mind
She says Wednesday afternoon would be just fine
I'm getting excited for I know we will share
Special time together in laughter and prayer

Kendra knows her Grammy will need some rest
And she wants to help care for me the very best
We agree to the time she will spend with us here
Until Saturday—it seems like a holiday so dear

I begin to plan some things we will do
And remember to log in some rest time too
Just thinking about her makes me smile
She truly is the most wonderful child

February 17th

It is Tuesday and already I'm getting excited
For Kendra will be here I am so delighted
Wilbur thinks this is such a good idea
He knows she will brighten my spirits and bring me cheer

I must pace myself and plan things with care
I must be careful and I do not dare
Do more than I can even though want to I may
I rest and try to keep the pain at bay

I fuss around the house picking up some clutter
And think I'm doing work and then I mutter
She's coming here to visit with us
She doesn't care is there is some dust

I call Amy to ask which sheets Kendra prefers
Regular or flannels; she tells me I'm spoiling her
I say that's my right as Kendra's Grandmother
She laughs and says you really are my Mother

I remind her the apple does not fall far from the tree
And this time she does not argue with me
We laugh at the thought that she has turned into her mother
Every daughter's nightmare in one way or another

But our love for each other has grown ever so strong
That we trust and know we can not do this wrong
Amy has turned out to be so much more than I dreamed
A daughter who loves me with both words and deeds

February 18th

It's Wednesday the day Kendra will come
I'm so excited I think I could run
Instead I do laundry and change the sheets
Flannel for us and flannel for my "sweets"

I manage to get some rest in today
I want to be strong for the next few days
I plan some outings I know she will adore
Like to her favorite place the local bookstore

I hear Wilbur drive up and my heart does pound
Kendra arrives and in the door she bounds
With hugs and kisses for Wilbur and me
She puts her things in her room with glee

For I have left "Bashful" the bear on her bed
With a note for her and she laughs in her head
How thoughtful she says as she comes down the stairs
I ask "what" like I have no idea about bears

It's Wilbur's night out and he's off to the gym
To meet with his friends and see who will win
The game of Wolleyball and who will pay
For the pizza and beer after the game they play

So it's dinner for two, just Kendra and me
A good time to relax and enjoy her company
She asks to say grace and I say yes to her appeal
She thanks God for Grammy, Wilbur her visit and her meal

February 19th

It's Thursday and Wilbur is home for today
He makes all of us breakfast and then we play
We spend time at the table having fun
And then we all go to the store for a quick run

We stop to see Doug who has asked to see Kendra
He greets her with hugs he's so loving and tender
We meet up with Wilbur at Stop & Shop
And then we head home—it is time to drop

Grammy needs a nap after lunch for I'm tired
So I go to bed feeling badly and begin the crying
Kendra comes up to speak softly with me
And stays with me until I fall asleep

She and Wilbur then do some research on line
For a project she's working on to finish on time
It's time spent well for each of us is aware
How much we can do and the need to prepare

Wilbur has asked Kendra what she would like for dinner
Shrimp with vegetables over pasta is her answer
I laugh out loud for I could predict this before
She can eat more shrimp than they have in the store

She asks to play a game and we let her pick
Monopoly is her choice so we set a time limit
We play until 9:30 the time we agree
She beats us both badly she is happy to be

It is off to bed for all of us now
She hugs and kisses us and tells us how
Grateful she is to have both of us near
We tell we are blessed for she is so dear

February 20th

It is Friday and Wilbur is away at work
Kendra reads her book and waits for me to wake
I get up a sleepyhead and we head downstairs
To make breakfast of bacon and grits to share

We each take a shower and get ready to go
We have places to visit and things to do
We stop at the Bank and I close an account
Then it's off to the bookstore to hunt around

I find what I'm looking for right at the start
Now Kendra looks on her own separate and apart
She finds her favorite author and calls me over to look
There are several to choose from of the many books

I purchase all four and she objects to the cost
She does not want Grammy to pay, but she is at a loss
For Grammy knows best that her love of books
Can only make her smarter—she gives me that look

She thanks me sincerely; we've had our time to play
Then we stop to see Joe in his office today
We surprise him and he is so happy we stopped by
To wish him luck for the New York Bar exam he's going to try

We head home to wait for Wilbur to greet
We've planned to have dinner out tonight, a special treat
We go to Chuck's and each order at will
But Kendra doesn't feel well and we fear she is ill

We wrap up her dinner for another day
She lies on the couch to watch Joan of Arcadia
We call her mom to say she's all right
And off we all go to bed for the night

February 21st

It's Saturday morning, the day that I dread
For later today off to home Kendra will head
We have a good breakfast and then we bake
For later tonight I have promised a cake

Wilbur is working at Camp Mohawk today
Doing volunteer work without any pay
He doesn't mind but he must be home by noon
To take Kendra to her basketball game by two

We stay for her game and watch her play well
Her team has been well coached it's easy to tell
They win by a score that is so lop-sided
We feel for the other team who loses quite badly

We kiss her goodbye and congratulate her win
And it is off to home to prepare for our game
For it's Trivia night and our turn to host
We scurry around and clean up the most

Wilbur cooks dinner while I take a rest
We have done all we can to prepare for our guests
The gang arrives and we eat, laugh and play
I must remember tonight not to forget to pray

I have had a spectacular few days
I am feeling tired but happy in ways
I've not felt for so long it seems like last fall
And it is then that I remember the beginning of the fall

The strain and stress and the pain of it all
Began in September, the beginning of fall
The job, the pain and trips for the tests
The doctor's visits and all of the rest

I am grateful and happy and feel very blessed
To have such good friends and the time to rest
The time to heal, recover and pray
For that I am grateful each and every day

February 22nd

It is Sunday and I take the time to sleep
Wilbur is in the barn across the street
I get up late and start to read the news
But I lose interest quickly for I have the blues

I miss our dear Kendra and can't put into words
The feelings I have for her fly in and out like the birds
I turn on my computer with intent to write and see
It is then that I see the message she left for me

She has left me a message of love that is so dear
Every time I turn on the computer her words will appear
What a blessing she is and I call her to tell
She says that she misses me too just as well

The day passes by very slowly and breezy
I turn on the TV and watch quite easily
Some old episodes of Law and Order
I'm not really interested I feel lonely and somber

I realize I've overstepped my limited agility
And I've pushed myself way too far past my ability
Wilbur comes in and asks if I want anything to eat
I tell him no, that I feel like defeat

He lovingly comes and sits by my side
And holds me close and allows me to cry
My tears of happiness and of distress
He knows how I feel without having to guess

February 23rd

It is Monday and a brand new week to begin
Wilbur is off to work away again
Later this afternoon he has a big interview
With a company that could change our entire point of view

He has work scheduled for the entire week
And another big interview set for next week
I flip over the calendar to see what's ahead for me
And the phone rings it is Dr. Spiegel to speak to me

He tells me by blood work is fine and okay
His call is just to check up on me and say
How am I feeling and to see if I've found
A way to gain some of the most needed pounds

I'm happy to know that he's thinking of me
And I report to him that a few pounds have indeed found me
He tells me I'm his hero and I laugh at the thought
That a Doctor like him knows I can be bought

A few words of praise and I'm smiling again
And then I am crying I am blessed to have him
As a Doctor who cares about his patients so much
I am humbled to tears and I am truly touched

I anxiously wait for Wilbur to arrive home again
To find out all about his day and then
To tell him how blessed and fortunate we are
To have each other to love and care for

February 24th

Today began slowly I'm sorry to say
I read way too long last night up until day
There must be a way to quiet my mind
Maybe sleeping with a hammer to hit me from behind

I climb into bed at about 4:30
And sleep until 10:00 before I am ready
To get up and face the world once again
There is pain in my joints and jello in my brain

The phone rings and I wait as long as I can
To muster up the courage to speak as I am
Still half asleep with coffee in hand
It is Kathy up the street to see how I am

I tell her I've had a great past few days
She wants to hear some of my writings of late
She thinks that I'm wonderful and encourages me
To keep at the writing, she knows just how to be

A great friend especially in my time of need
I'll use her as an editor, the entire book to read
Perhaps I will feed it to her month by month
Or else she may want to eat it for lunch

I'm happy to have her as good friend and neighbor
She and Ed have so much life and love to savor
They share what they have and do such good deeds
There must be a place in heaven for folks such as these

February 25th

Today I awake nervous unable to speak
A new therapist I'm going to meet
What will she think of this mess that I'm in?
I'm anxious to go and then frightened again

I meet her exactly at the allotted time
And find her to be both gracious and kind
We share a few laughs and in minutes she knows
For my independence jumps out and really shows

We have a good visit, better than I expect
And set up a time to meet again next
I then go about the errands I have set
To deliver some gifts which have not been sent yet

I come home quite pleased and proud of myself
For I've conquered some fears and sought some new help
I feel pretty good in not too much pain
I relax for I have just unloaded my brain

I wait for Wilbur to come home this night
I want to tell him some hope is in sight
He is happy to hear all about my day
And is proud of me too in his own special way

February 26th

It is Thursday and I sleep in for a while
I finish my new book and rest with a smile
I'm careful to not plan too much for the day
For tonight we will go to see Kendra play

The semi-final playoff is what is at stake
We are cheering her on and are wide awake
Her team wins the game and now they will play
The final playoff game I'm excited to say

Kendra has just gotten a new hair cut
I ask the coach just how did he get
Halle Berry to come and play on his team
He smiles and tells me she looks like a dream

She is playing the game with much more spirit
They've been very well coached and she loves every minute
We hug her good-bye and express our love
Once again to heaven for our angel sent from above

February 27th

It is Friday the day I take my Fosamax
To strengthen by bones, what little is left
I take the day slowly and talk for a while
Then do some laundry and fold up the piles

Amy phones to say she will pick me up
Tomorrow at around eleven o'clock
I'll spend the day with them; I'm delighted beyond reason
I'll get to see Kendra play her final game of the season

Wilbur will be helping his mother to move
To a brand new place, I hope it goes smooth
His sister and brother-in-law will be there to assist
Along with the moving crew she has enlisted

I've taken some pain meds and now I must rest
To save up my energy for tomorrow's big test
To see if I can really stay awake all day long
I know in my heart tomorrow will be like a song

To spend the entire day with those I love dearly
Will be so wonderful, I'm already getting teary
Wilbur will pick me up and drive me along
To our sweet little nest, the place we call home

February 28th

This morning Amy drives out this long way
To pick me up for the events of the day
We stop at the mall to have Kendra's hair done
By a real professional, 2 ½ hours before she is done

She looks quite beautiful to say the least
And now she's going to sweat like a beast
This is the final playoff game for her team
There are many fans there but she doesn't seem

The least bit scared or afraid to play
For now it is trophy time and we all yell yeah
The game is a tough one they start out ahead
But the second half slows down and it is neck in neck

The game is over and they finally achieve
The goal that they wanted and each really believed
The coaches are pleased and each girl is called
Separately by name to receive their award

Two trophies are given and each is special
They did not think it possible to win this year's session
But champions they are and they each deserve
The applause they receive by all that observe

It's a trying day for me; I've had no time to rest
And when we arrive home I'm weary at best
I take some pain meds to take off the edge
And then I head quickly right to my bed

February 29th

An extra day we've been given this year
To do as we please it seems so dear
An entire 24 hours are given as a gift
But I am very tired so through catalogues I sift

I over-extended just once again
But I knew that the price would be extra pain
I wanted so badly to be at the game
For Kendra and her team it was worth the pain

So I am resting until later today and I yawn
When we will go down town to visit with Lynn and John
Our very dear friends from the seminar we attended
Last summer when we were luckily befriended

These people are so dear and so very giving
They have just finished another 4-day seminar about really living
They give of themselves and then they give more
With lessons to learn for us to keep in store

For the rest of our lives to put into practice
To deal with the difficult and not be distracted
But to focus instead on the good things together
By the love and respect we each have for one another

March 1st

A lazy day I awake again in pain
But it is sunny outside and I begin to plan
How soon it will be before I can go
And plant outside when there finally is no snow

March is here and it is fairly warm by chance
But we all know not to be fooled by March's dance
She can shed sunshine and then again snow
It is a difficult month but one that I know

Is a good time for dreaming about warmer weather
When we can go outside simply wearing a sweater
Without all the coats, the boots and the hats
And simply relax for awhile perhaps take a nap

In the warm sunshine God sends from above
He knows we've all had enough of the cold winter snow
All the plant and seed catalogs arrive in the mail
Thank God for the flowers some bright; others pale

My mind is healing but my body is slow
I am still very chilled looking out at the snow
I know it is melting but not fast enough
It is like my body both frail and tough

March 2nd

It is Tuesday and I awake not too tired
I want to go play in the garden outside
But there remains too much snow on the ground
When will it all melt and let us design around?

The gardens have hopefully made it through the cold
It is difficult to tell we have not seen a bulb
Peeking through the snow and the good ground cover
Perhaps they're afraid to peek out and discover

That the sun is not warming the ground enough yet
To allow us to see signs of growth but I bet
They are anxious to pop their little heads up
To smile at us softly with each little bud

It's been a long winter, that is for sure
And everyone is waiting for the skies of azure
And the colors of early flowers all yellow and pretty
Please hurry God and on us take pity

March 3rd

It's a very glum day and I stay in bed
I'm angry and don't want anything, enough said
I stay under the covers, safe and warm
With little Miss Ella to keep me calm

What ever is the matter with me?
I try but I don't understand
I recognize the pain, which is nothing new
Yet I still feel nothing but blue

Has the pain I feel really gotten so bad?
That I don't even know anymore
What it's like to not feel the pain every day
And so I've closed the door, forgotten to pray?

That's not the future I'm looking for
There is much too much at stake
And so I spend some time in thought and prayer
Then sleep for a while, what a day!

I wake up more peaceful and I truly know why
My body has slowed down for a while
But my brain does not so easily shut down
So I work at reading the good words, which are around

March 4th

It's Thursday the day for my visit to Doug
For a haircut and color to cheer up this mug
But I arrive too early, I think it's eleven
And that's when I learn it's at one

So I return home to take a quick nap
Feeling really stupid and quite like a sap
But the time is spent really well I think
I rest, eat, and have something to drink

I return at one the allotted time
And Doug greets me with a laugh and a hug
He understands at once how I made the mistake
And I laugh at myself while my brain takes a break

We are finally finished and laugh all the while
Doug is such a good joker and friend
He makes me feel like a princess again
So as I'm leaving, I wave my wand

March 5th

It's the day for my visit to the new therapist
This is the second time and I am still nervous
I wonder what she really thinks of me
I'm not there for her, I am there for me

She is extremely good at gleaning out stuff
I thought was unimportant and more or less useless
But she winds it together to learn more and more
About the family and me which came before

I am very trusting and speak with ease
She is as comfortable as can be
She asks the right questions and gives me the time
To think and ponder about this and another time

She digs like an archeologist with hope to find
What lies beneath and within me so blind
She is very adept as the process takes place
That I am almost unaware that this is a case

I feel better upon leaving and think when we end
That I'm enjoying the process and can't wait to find
What is really locked up and why that is so?
I am thankful to God for the chance to go

March 6th

We went dancing last night and today I am spent
We also did shop in a store with a floor of cement
My feet hurt, my joints and also my spine
Are in severe trauma, so I lay sublime

In my sweet little bed I spend most of the day
It is windy and damp so I read and play
I flip through the catalogues for my grandsons
And order the things as requested by their mom

Alayne is so practical at times it's safe to say
That she has little room in her life for fun and play
Ethan and Graham are just little boys
They need more of her time, not more toys

And so I comply with my daughter's wishes
And purchase the gifts she has on her lists
It seems much more fun to pick out from home
The things I know they would like to own

We'll see them on Monday at Ethan's concert
We are excited to hear him play his trumpet
He seems to possess the natural gift
Of music, which to us is a wonderful lift

We haven't seen much of the boys of late
They are growing like trees so tall and straight
I wish things were smoother with my daughter and her mother
But when I try it seems useless and I think—why bother?

Her calls are so seldom and never to see
How I am doing or what's new with me
She calls to inform us of the boy's needs and events
And if we have time could we possibly attend

March 7th

It is Sunday, the day of rest once again
As we await the beginning of the big game
The UCONN women and the UCONN men
Both play at 2:00, this is nuts, who scheduled them?

The women have won their quarterfinal game
And now tomorrow they must play
Against Boston College whom they've played before
Let's hope that this time UCONN will out-score

The men have lost against the Syracuse team
A real shame due to a major player's injury
But they'll be back to play again
And next time they are sure to win

Kendra just called me to see how I am
And to tell me about her team's pizza party
And when that was over, with all her fatigue
She went to try out and play for another league

I'm truly delighted whenever she phones
She has completed the book that we brought home
The one the bookstore asked her to read and critique
She rated it 5 stars and wrote in her unique

Way in the spaces provided for her to tell
Just how good the book was and she rated it well
She is anxious to do this project again
It allows her to read books prior to publishing of them

Now I am tired and in need of some meds
So it is off to the kitchen I go
For a glass of lemonade to sip
And put the pain away for a bit

March 8th

I'm beginning to understand more about my mother
And the reasons she did things her way
It is not that she loved me less than my brother
It's just the way things were done in her day

She spent time in the kitchen and more time on chores
It appeared to me to be very obsessive
But to her there weren't any other choices
She simply went about doing things just to live

It's funny to look back in retrospect
And realize the impact it had
I learned to take responsibility with its affect
While my brother always seemed a little bit sad

Our interests were usually quite different than our genders
With his main focus on flowers and music
While I took the avenue of sports and bending
With acrobatics and writing anything artistic

It seems that I was Daddy's little girl
All the while being his son
And my brother was my mother's little boy
Playing quietly out in the sun

Now that we're grown up and our parents long gone
We have great love and respect for each other
But it took a long time for this realization to come
We are now truly sister and brother

I thank God for Bert and his place in my life
And I know that he feels the same
For he is there to comfort me in strife
And I am always there ready for him

March 9th

The beginning of the week, a good time for me
For I have not pushed too far
Over the weekend I rested and read
And wished upon a star

To gain understanding and make some sense
Of all this pain I'm going through
The lesson I'm learning is to finally slow down
And let my real light shine through

Tonight is Ethan's concert at six
We are all excited to go
To take advantage of each opportunity
That is given to us and to know

How dearly each gift is handed to us
Along this path that we travel
And be grateful for each and every time
We are given a new chance to marvel

At those all around us we take for granted
But seldom take the time to say
How much they are loved and needed by us
Why do we hold back—are we afraid?

March 10th

I'm learning so much and at such a fast pace
It is hard for me to keep up
With all the lessons of each new day
Which push me along and yet

The learning is tough and I'm beginning to see
That life can be good no matter what
For each of us has our own load to bear
It is why we are here; forget that not

It is said that a little adversity
Is a very good thing for man
For kites rise against not with the wind
Just how much does God have in mind?

I think of them as stumbling blocks
But that is not what they are
If I stack them up upon each other
I may be able to reach a star

If you dump a box of blocks on the floor
And invite the children to play
You will certainly see that creativity
Is the lesson to learn for the day

We see these blocks as adversity
To step over, go around or get the key
When really they are truly God's gift to us
To challenge our minds and set us free

March 11th

Snow has fallen upon us again
And we are reminded once more
That God has His own timetable for us
We are all hoping for Spring that's for sure

But we are asked with patience to wait
For warm weather to make its appearance
Snow is beautiful in December we say
But in March we wish for good riddance

Here we are once again living life in a hurry
Not appreciating the time we are given
For when the warm weather finally arrives
We will think we are really in heaven

Why is it so difficult for us to wait
Is it that we have grown so impatient?
Or are we just spoiled with instant things
That we no longer have the patience?

Please bless me today with the patience I need
To help me endure this process
Of disease and treatment I must go through
To be more of a person not less

March 12th

I wrote a note to Ethan today
To tell him how much we enjoyed
The wonderful concert we did attend
And that we were truly overjoyed

To have him as our oldest grandson
And to witness the talent he's acquired
Not only to play his trumpet so well
But also his singing in the choir

We truly were impressed with all that we saw
The town's schools all joining together
To perform a concert for all to enjoy
Despite the terrible weather

Ethan really has the musical ability
That seems in the family to run
And he is eager to perform for us
We just need to ask him and it's done

I do not remember having that special gift
Of someone to go to in need
That unique quality that grandparents have
To spoil each child with love and deed

God bless our children and their children
For they learn so much from their parents
We are graced and blessed for each of them
Is so special to us, their grandparents

March 13th

Today is a special day indeed
It is my friend Kathy's birthday
A day to celebrate life at its best
To dance, be merry and gay

I have been blessed to know and have her
As both good neighbor and friend
She has shown me what friendship really means
We will remain friends to the end

She has been there for me throughout this ordeal
With words of encouragement and praise
She has fed me the most exquisite custard
When I had not eaten for days

God bless her with grace from up above
She has earned a place in heaven
She gives of her time and of herself
In ways beyond comprehension

And so I have chosen a special gift
Because she has become so dear
Without her I would not be able to continue on
She helps carry the burdens I bear

March 14th

Dear Cory

Dear daughter of mine I want you to know
You are loved more than you'll ever believe
And I am so sorry to learn of your news
Of loss and sorrow and grief

I'm sure you have heard every platitude there exists
That you can try once again
But nothing erases the memory of such loss
And the feeling of terrible pain

I carry your burden with me each day
And hope it lessens the grief
To know someone else is sharing your pain
And that somehow you find some relief

I know you have great neighbors and friends
And that is certainly good news
Please reach out to them in your time of need
They will help ease the feeling of blues

I wish we were closer to visit you
To bring you some laughter and cheer
But the distance is too far for us to come now
We can simply pray from here

Good things are in store for you I'm sure
You have been such a good friend for me
The healing and mending take their own sweet time
Please be patient and you will see

I wish you and Mark the best of times
With pleasant and long memories

I love you so much, I can hardly write
Without crying out loud with my tears

Spring is coming, but not fast enough
We are tired of snow and cold
But soon the flowers will begin to bloom
And provide hope for us all to hold

March 15th

Our granddaughter Kendra has done it again
She continues to amaze us all
She tried out herself for an AAU league
And was accepted to play basketball

She did not invite nor tell any of her friends
She simply went out by herself alone
I can hardly believe that she had the courage
And confidence to go it alone

Congratulations to her for at the age of twelve
I am not aware of too many
Who would dare to try-out all by themselves
And not bring a friend to accompany

She has gained quite a bit of knowledge this year
And expect she will learn much more
About the game and all the plays
That will lead to a winning score

She called to tell me she was accepted
And that she was very proud
I can't wait for her to play her very first game
So I can be there to shout out loud!!!!

March 16th

I continue to learn about the women in my life
Beginning with my dear mother
And all of her sisters except for Molly
Who loved me more than the others

I have two daughters of my own
And a step-daughter whom I love
But all has not always gone so well
And so begins the testing from above

The piano teacher whom I called "Aunt Rose"
Who was by mother's good friend
Turned out to be my abuser instead
And destroyed my trust to the end

I finally gave up the piano for good
And nobody could believe that I quit
For it seemed that I did possess real talent
But the price that I paid was too great

What choice did I have as a molested child?
I drew back into myself fragile and frail
And never again dared to touch the piano
Afraid I would remember the trail

Of quiet tears and solitude
That nobody would believe
How is that someone in whom I trusted
Could lie to me and deceive?

The tapestry woven of women in my life
Is filled with mistrust and deceit
I must find a way to reweave the threads
So that I can live my life complete

March 17th

The pattern continues to repeat itself
When I began my career in legal and banking
I was unable to trust most women in general
They seemed more interested in gossip than working

My career took off because I was smart
In a time when it was not cool
Most of the women were pretty and coy
But I was a working fool

Project after project was given to me
And the promotions that go with them too
I climbed the ladder and made myself
Indispensable because I could

Most men that I worked with applauded me
For achieving the top of the dome
But women chattered behind my back
They could not believe I made it on my own

What is the reward for hard work today?
I wonder how it all plays out?
For I am no longer able to work
And I'm grateful to call a time-out

March 18th

I'm beginning to see the pattern clearly now
So deeply woven in scars
I placed my trust in too many wrong places
I may as well have wished on a star

But now I have time to pause and reflect
On the many reasons now known
Partly of why I've been so sick
And of the things I've not wanted to own

Healing takes time from long lasting wounds
Inflicted such a long time ago
But through prayer and study I'm ready to learn
And realize I've a long way to go

I'm still in pain mostly physically
Which is how my body reacts
It breaks down in time to save itself
And me from a total relapse

I'm happy to be and continue to grow
We just looked at a new piano to buy
I refuse to let the past rule my life
I will play again—I will not be denied!!!!!

March 19th

It is Friday today the 19th of March
Spring will be here in just a few days
It's been snowing for 3 days straight in a row
A winter wonderland everything is glazed

The ground is covered in fairly deep snow
And soon there will be lots of mud
The woodstove is keeping me warm and dry
But my heart is longing to see rose buds

We are going to have dinner at Alayne's tonight
To celebrate Ethan's and Brian's birthdays
It will be fun to have pizza with the entire gang
As Amy and clan will be there too—oh yeah!

The pain monster is rearing its ugly head
I'm sure it's because of the weather
I'm trying to stay just one step ahead
And am learning to control it much better

To say that I'm still quite overwhelmed
Would be an understatement at best
But I am learning albeit so slowly
To live more fully and in myself to place trust

March 20th

Wilbur is working in his shop this morning
Cleaning and organizing his wares
I awake and find a fire is glowing
In the kitchen woodstove downstairs

It is a quiet day after yesterday's chaos
I seem to dislike celebrations
There is too much noise and too many comments
And way too many expectations

The girls have a great difference of opinion
On exactly how their children should be raised
We have witnessed this a great many times
And it always leaves us quite crazed

What happens next—the stress is too much
And my body wants to recoil
The body stiffens the pain sets in
And leaves me in great turmoil

I try to take it easy today
And give myself time to recover
The pain meds do help and so does some sleep
I am glad this event is over

March 21st

It is Sunday again and I find myself weeping
For no apparent reason at all
The therapist and I are reaching very deep
To what lies at my deepest core

We have uncovered some things that I'd rather forget
But the memories are becoming much clearer
And though I wish they were not mine
I'm learning to search even deeper

I'm feeling both fragile and strong today
A paradox beyond my control
I want to be strong and face the world
And then again perhaps crawl into a hole

I know that when the process is done
I will have lived through a thousand years
Some happy, some sad, some gentle, some harsh
And I will have cried one million tears

But tomorrow will come
And with it new hope
With renewed body, spirit and mind
I will truly be able to cope

March 22nd

I'm off to see Dr. Spiegel today
I think he will be very pleased
For I've put on at least a few new pounds
And I'm proud of the way that I feel

It's six pounds exactly when I am weighed in
And we are both pleasantly surprised
He now knows I've made the solid connection
Between the body, the soul and the mind

I visit some close friends at the bank
My former boss greets me with glee
I know after spending just one hour's time
I could not return there, this I see

The entire place is in total chaos
The morale is exceptionally low
Management really does not exist
As the work force races to and fro

I go to the bookstore to return Kendra's book
And look for some new things to read
It is easy to find the books that I like
My selection is made with ease

It's home for some chores and then for a rest
It has been a very busy day
I loved having the chance to go outside
To go browsing around and to play

March 23rd

Yesterday was more taxing than I thought
So today I took time to sleep
I've managed to do two loads of laundry
Which for me is a tremendous feat

I'm going to aerobics for the first time tonight
I'm excited beyond belief
I know that just moving around a bit
Will bring my body much needed relief

I will work on the floor not using a step
I want to feel some success
I know not to push my body too far
Or I'll end up feeling distress

It's been a long time coming this feeling I have
Of once again being complete
Just being and doing the person I am
Not having to win or compete

The pain still exists but not to the degree
That puts me in total despair
But I will remain cautious because I know
It can return simply out of thin air

I'm much more in control than I've been for a while
But still too weak to return to my job
That is just fine with be because
Time is precious and I won't be robbed

March 24th

I sleep in late; I'm a little bit tired
Yesterday's workout took more energy than I had
But I went very slowly, wanting to be safe
It was the right thing to do as I left feeling glad

Just to move by body again
Was such a big thrill to me
I must continue to monitor my speed
Until I am completely free

The therapist's visit went very well
She said that I was very strong indeed
She understands and believes in me
As I'm learning to pace myself by need

I left feeling quite happy to be
Myself and not such a failure
I continue to learn more about me
I accept my strength and people who nurture

To know how to pace myself even though
I want the process to go faster
Is evidence that I now accept and do believe
That my life is not a total disaster

I've not taken paid meds in two days now
And my muscles are a little bit sore
But if I can control the pain with my mind
I'll be that much ahead to be sure

March 25th

It is damp and cold and dreary today
I expected to see the warm sun
I went to get my haircut again
The place is such a source of fun

I so much enjoy the time spent there
Everyone jokes and cares for me
I always leave ever so happy and pleased
As though I was part of the family

The rest of the day is devoted to laundry
It is really quite a simple chore
A task that I am now able to manage
And one I look forward to more and more

Just to clean up the kitchen or run an errand
Is truly a delight you see
Not wanting to stay in bed all day long
Has shown me a brand new me

I look forward to class again tonight
And I promise to go at a slow pace
For I now know that running too fast
Will land me smack on my face

Tomorrow promises sunshine and warmth
A day to look forward to
The piano is scheduled to me here by morning
And I will be playing by two

March 26th

It is Friday morning and I am up early
I can barely believe what's to come
The piano arrives just at the right time
And I sit and am playing by one

Next is a trip to the Naturopath
One I'm looking forward to
Michelle says I'm making fairly good progress
And she says I am also looking good

We talk for a while and she gathers more input
To prescribe what she has in mind
I take her instructions with me as I leave
She truly is understanding and kind

I come home and sit and play for a while
My fingers are not used to this
But no matter how bad the notes I miss
The music to me is bliss

March 27th

It is Saturday morning and again I wake early
Wilbur is out working in the barn
I'm going to meet Amy and Kendra
To watch my little basketball star

It is just a scrimmage and learning new plays
And Kendra is catching on so fast
I'm so happy to be there because now I can go
More places than I have in the past

I return home to bake the promised lemon cake
That we will take along for our game of trivia
I rest for a while and watch some TV
Basketball is all over the media

When we return home I am aching and sore
It is then that I realize too late
That I have been pushing the entire week
And now I really need a break

We retire to bed but I do not sleep
The pain monster is growling quite loud
I put on the pain patches to get some relief
I should take the meds but I'm too proud

Sleep finally comes after quite a long time
Of laying awake and being in pain
I know that I've pushed myself way too far
I vow not to do that again

March 28th

Sunday is here and I sleep until noon
It's a good thing that Granny has called
To say she is not up to company today
Because I am really feeling appalled

My body is tired and I have no strength
I'm paying the price for last week
I must remember to not over-do
Or else I'll really end up quite weak

I take it easy for the rest of the day
Doing some reading and watching TV
I feel so let down because I neglected
To take care of little old me

We go to bed early and I sleep very well
I've learned an important lesson indeed
I can no longer push myself beyond the point
Even though it is what I want and think I need

March 29th

Monday is here am I'm feeling renewed
I tackle quite a few chores
I rest in between because now I know
That I must learn to close the doors

The rest will always be waiting for me
When I awake from my nap
I feel rested and fueled with new energy
And am grateful to have learned from that

I begin again with the rest of the things
I wanted to accomplish today
I am quite happy and proud of myself
For I'm learning a lot of new ways

To allot some time for work and then to rest
Is a brand new experience for me
I used to be able to rush right in
And tackle just about anything you see

March 30th

I did not sleep very well last night
So I went up to the loft to read
Wilbur had an early flight to catch
And the bed was really his need

His snoring was loud and I do expect
That he was nervous about the day ahead
I finally fell asleep up in the loft
But awoke too early and went back to bed

I got up, had coffee and read for a bit
Before resting again
Then it was laundry and food for myself
So that I could avoid the pain

I was successful in paying attention
To what my body was saying
I did not over-do and so I'm glad
I can go to aerobics without paying

I've fueled my body for tonight's workout
And hope that I can keep up the pace
Although moving slowly, I'm finally learning
To accept my limitations with grace

March 31st

It is a cold and rainy morning today
It does not feel much like spring
I'm feeling much better than I have in days
And I want to play piano and sing

My strength is returning albeit so slowly
And I am pleased for that means
That I will be able to accomplish much more
Go places and do many things

It is the end of March this day
Although it looks like November
But I am determined to keep the faith
And know how to pray and remember

That better days are indeed ahead
I am truly grateful and understand
The pain is not too awful today
Despite the weather at hand

I find that my spirit is much improved
And I thank God each and every day
For the wonderful blessings that He has bestowed
That I witness in so many different ways

Family and friends and former co-workers
Who call and ask how I'm getting along
That people in general can know and love me
And still make me feel that I belong

April 1st

It is the first of April and no sign of spring
Mother Nature has fooled us once again
Ella has curled up on by bed inside
And I want to curl up beside her and hide

But it's off to the doctor I go for a check-up
To monitor my progress, thank goodness there is some
Enough to be measured in weight and how I look
My spirit is high and I continue with my book

The doctor is pleased and we talk for a while
She asks many questions and offers her smile
I know from her look that she is genuine and sincere
She asks again if the pain is still so severe

I tell her it comes and goes without warning
But she knows that I push too hard and need calming
I mention the weather and how it affects me
She answers that that's when I should take it easy

I want so much to be normal like others
But need to accept the pain and the bothers
I know that my spirit of mind has control
To lessen the pain if I only let go

I work all day long at cleaning out closets
And manage to package thirteen boxes
To take to Goodwill for someone else to wear
My goodness my closets all seem to look bare

I know I need rest and protein to eat
So I rest for a while and pick up my feet
And then go to class to move all around
And then home to sleep safely and sound

April 2nd

It continues to be cold and very dismal
The weather outside is truly abysmal
My body is stiff and in much pain
I pushed too far yesterday and now I must pay

I'm taking it easy not doing too much to tell
Although the spring cleaning bug is alive and well
I know I must wait to complete the job
And I find that the waiting is extremely hard

I spoke with my brother for a short little chat
It seems that he is also suffering with his back
I tell him about the patches of Lidoderm
And he promises to call his doctor in return

We want very much to attend his concert
But it will become difficult if I still hurt
He understands well and says not to worry
I want to do everything and in quite a hurry

It's patience I'm praying for most of all
I must remember to heed God's call
This lesson of pain is teaching me much
In fact I think enough is enough

I'll rest for the remainder of the day
Because tonight I want to go play
To hear good music and have the chance
To get out on the floor perhaps to dance!!!!!!

April 3rd

We did not go out to dance last night
To stay in and rest seemed to be right
This morning we get up early to attend
Graham's First Communion, my choice is to bend

We arrive at Alayne's in plenty of time
And everything seems to be going just fine
But nothing pleases her and she throws me a jab
I refuse to answer, but it does make me mad

Graham looks so handsome in his white shirt and tie
He is so sensitive and almost seems shy
I'm certain his mother has lectured him well
As to how to behave and just what to tell

The Mass is over and we return for lunch
His other grandparents are there, what a happy bunch
We eat and then Graham opens his gifts
He is quite pleased with the presents he lifts

For each of us to see that he is so proud
We all love him so and applaud out loud
The tension is still there is seems to loom
Around the house from room to room

We finally bid farewell and I'm already in pain
From sitting too long just once again
We now head to Hartford to the designated place
Where we can see Kendra play her first AAU game

Amy has purchased a padded seat with a backrest
So I will be comfortable sitting, she is the best
We watch the game and cheer the team on
And then head for home and turn the TV on

To watch the UCONN men play and beat Duke
What a surprise, is it merely a fluke?
We go to bed tired and I sob myself to sleep
I've done too much today, I should crawl before I leap

April 4th

It is Sunday morning and I sleep in late
The beginning of Daylight Saving Time has begun
We lost an hour of sleep last night
But I'm over-tired because I've over-done

So Wilbur goes alone to visit his mother
I really want to go with him but know much better
I do a few chores and rest for the day
Hoping to recover and become a go-getter

We stay up to watch the UCONN women play
And defeat their opponent what glorious fun
Both the men and the women are in the finals
And we are anxious to see if both teams will run

If they both win their games it will be the first time
Two teams from the same school bring home the win
All of the state is cheering both teams on
We want this piece of history—we are all a-kin

We retire to bed very happy for them
I have taken my meds to ward off the pain
Tomorrow is therapy early in the morning
And I thank God for all of my blessings again

April 5th

It is off to the therapist this morning I go
The weather feels like it's twenty below
The wind is howling and it is really cold
Just to go outside I feel very bold

Our meeting goes well and I am improving
I still need to adjust to the world I'm living
It is so different from working all day
I sometimes forget that this is not play

It's truly recovery and nothing more
My body continues to be achy and sore
I must pay attention to every sign I get
Or I'll have a relapse and be back in bed

I go to the clothes store after our meeting
There are great sales I find some good things
Finally I now have some clothing that fits me
That doesn't look like a bag hanging on a tree

I have something to eat when I return home
And speak with by brother awhile on the phone
Amy calls to give me some unpleasant news
And I wish her good luck and do not refuse

To help her out in any way that I'm able
I know my limits and of what I am capable
She thanks me for listening; I'm the fortunate one
She trusts and loves me and soon we'll have fun

In just two weeks time we'll travel together
To stay in Rhode Island, what could be better?
For Amy, Kendra, Olivia and me
To go play and watch basketball, be happy and free

April 6th

The news is in, the men have won
The championship game is theirs to claim
UCONN is one happy place to be
They have earned their honors and fame

The women play tonight and if they win
History will be made in college ball
For never before have two teams won
From the same school ever before

The entire state is excited for them
Even those who don't follow the sport
Everywhere you go you see UCONN flags
Waving proudly from everyone's porch

Following the game has caused loss of sleep
I try to take naps during the day
But sleep eludes me and I stay awake
I want to watch every single play

April 7th

The women have won—history is made
The TV is full of good news
The papers have pictures of the entire teams
The state has erupted in white and blue

A parade is planned to honor both teams
The players, the coaches and fans
This is truly amazing, people are cheering
They line the streets in cars and vans

I am thoroughly exhausted in body and mind
Lack of sleep is definitely the cause
There is national coverage on the TV news
And I don't want to miss it or pause

I will sleep well tonight—of this I am sure
Basketball has taken its toll
By body is sore and my back is on fire
I must relax both my body and soul

April 8th

It is Thursday the night for aerobics class
But I am as whipped as can be
So I stay at home, read and rest
And then watch a little TV

Amy calls to tell me that Olivia is sick
She's been throwing up since early Tuesday
Unfortunately I can do nothing to help
I need to rest myself and have this day

She understands, but I feel some regret
That I am not able to help out
Why can't I be just a little bit stronger?
I wish there were another way out

It's Holy Thursday and I am remembering
The times from not so long ago past
When the family would gather around the table
Have bread and wine for dinner and then begin the fast

I find that I miss the old traditions
The one's that surround Holy Week
Especially the Thursday tradition
And the washing of the feet

This week is hell for my dear brother Bert
He spends time at church the entire week
His back is not good and he is in pain
But he carries on for this week in the Church is its peak

April 9th

It is Good Friday, what a crazy name
For the day our good Lord did die
It certainly was not very good for him
I guess the good is for you and I

I'm still feeling pain all over my body
There isn't a place that is free
The lack of sleep has finally caught up
And is teaching a lesson to me

I call to see how Olivia is doing
And check on Kendra as well
Amy is in way over her head
A mother always can tell

I ask her if it would be all right
To bring Easter dinner to them
She says that would be wonderful
She wants to see us both again

I take my pain meds and finally sleep
Hoping to feel better tomorrow
I have too many things on my mind
And a lot of it is Amy's sorrow

April 10th

I sleep pretty soundly through the night
And wake up with some energy
I go out and shop for Easter things
For Wilbur and Amy's family

The shopping goes well and I return home
And manage to get the gifts wrapped
And then I get myself something to eat
Lie down and take a long nap

Wilbur is out working in the barn
On a beautiful bench what a wonder
It is made out of cherry and is quite unique
It will be the perfect spot to sit and ponder

I think he will put it near the rose garden
Which is dedicated to those we've lost and loved
There are separate bushes each with a marker
This garden is blessed from above

The smallest bush, the one for my mother
Grows taller and taller each year
It is as though she is sprinkling her love
To make sure it survives by her tears

I love the idea of the memorial rose garden
It gives us a chance to pray and remember
For each time we look outside we can see
Each and every family member

April 11th

Easter Sunday is here but the weather is cold
It is far from bright and sunny
I sneak down the stairs to place Wilbur's gift
And find a beautiful Easter bunny

I will not be able to wear what I planned
Who cares I will be safe and warm
We load up the car and head down the road
To Amy's place with hopes to keep them from harm

Carlos has been gone for a few weeks now
It was at the counselor's suggestion
That they separate from each other for a while
And that Carlos gets some clear direction

He is at his mother's house now
And life for all is a wreck
Amy has the entire burden on herself
And she is about to break

I think she needs some counseling herself
And also for Kendra and Olivia
Olivia is acting out in strange ways
While Kendra becomes more silent day by day

Their struggles are causing me much heartache and pain
I know they must work things out
For each of them is entitled to live happily
So I pray and then I pray and shout

God are you listening, it's me again
But this time the prayers are not for me
They are for Amy & Carlos, Kendra and Olivia
My God they are my true family

April 12th

Wilbur is quite concerned about me
I'm much too quiet again
He knows my heart is breaking in half
And that it causes me to be in pain

I spend the entire day reading a book
It keeps me from thinking too much
My mind is otherwise occupied for a time
I even forget to have lunch

It is not good for me to miss a meal
In fact I should eat every two hours
But today I could care less about eating at all
I want to see sunshine and flowers

By late afternoon my belly begins to hurt
And I realize what I have done
So I take a break and get something to eat
I feel quite stupid and dumb

Wilbur makes his famous rice dish for dinner
And I eat a very small bowl
My stomach hurts and I am in pain
I want to crawl into a hole

I make some progress and then slide back
I'm supposed to make steady progress
I can't tolerate the way I look and feel
This disease is truly hideous

April 13th

My mood has changed; I'm feeling quite glum
It is cold and rainy outside
Everyone I know is sick with something
I need to feel more hope inside

I'll plan to rest for most of the day
And go to aerobics tonight
Perhaps just getting out and moving around
Will help my attitude be a little more bright

It's hard to maintain a bright attitude
When the weather feels like November
We really need some sunshine and warmth
I've forgotten what it's like and can't remember

Nothing is green and the trees are still bare
It feels more like fall than spring
I long to take my bike out for a ride
With Wilbur beside me and bells to ring

I look forward to Saturday and lunch with the girls
They are coming to take me out
They think that we're just going to lunch
But I need to be out and about

I've not ventured too far from home these days
I sometimes can't believe this is really me
For never before was I content to be home
To do as I please and be free

April 14th

Today is Wilbur's big interview
With Advest, a company in Hartford
I know in my heart he does not want to give up
His free enterprise company for good

But money is scarce and the future promises few
Though everyone loves his work
Unless they are willing to pay for it
The family finances are beginning to hurt

Aerobics went quite awful last night
I had no get up and go
And so I was forced to rest in between
The exercises and take it very slow

It seems like I take three forward steps
And then take two in reverse
The pain is quite intense today
Somehow this feels like a curse

I know that I have too much on my mind
And that I must truly let go
Let God take over my burdens somehow
And trust in Him, have faith and say so

Talk is easy but difficult to mind
But I really do believe
That when I let go and pray some more
That I will find real relief

April 15th

The dreaded tax day has finally arrived
And we are no different than most folks
Although they've been prepared for a while
We wait to send in our last bucks

Money is scarce and a source of worry
I'm hoping my disability pay will continue
Unless Wilbur gets this new job he wants
There will be little to serve on the menu

The day began in the usual way
I awoke and had breakfast to eat
I fueled my body all day long
So that aerobics would not mean defeat

I did quite well keeping up with the class
It is difficult for me to build strength
My ligaments and tendons are so very long
Although limber my limbs are too long in length

And so I work harder and feel the burn
As my weak muscles struggle to form
It does seem so odd to be limber and yet
At the same time not to be strong

I come home tired and take a shower
My body is aching all over
I know that I must continue this path
If I truly intend to recover

The day ends well and before I rest
I take my meds and grab a treat
Wilbur and I talk for a while
Then we head off to bed to get some sleep

April 16th

Today is Friday and Fosamax day
The drug I take to strengthen my bones
It gives me the world's worst stomachache
But somehow I struggle along

I send Kendra a card today
Because she's having a hard time
I tell her that I love her so much
And that she can call me anytime

I also send Amy a card to tell her
That I love her and to keep up her courage
Carlos has caused so much pain in their lives
He has brought so much extra baggage

He is going for counseling once a week now
But he's not doing it for himself, which would be right
He thinks that by simply attending the sessions
That Amy will allow him back in her life

She has taken him back two times already
It is time now to move along forward
She must re-establish a life with the girls
And not be fooled by Carlos the coward

This situation causes me much stress
And I know that my pain is increased
I try to listen as much as I'm able
But know my health must come first

So I continue to pray without any motive
Except to accept what is to come
I hope that I have the courage I need
And the strength that I'll need to call from

April 17th

Today was one of my best days ever
The girls and I met for lunch
Then we went shopping together for fun
What a happy delightful bunch

We shared some good laughs with each other
And told stories about life at work
I'm so glad not to be there at all
The place sounds as if it's gone berserk

The day goes by quickly, too quickly for me
As we travel from shop to shop
I'm having quite a delightful time
I don't want the time for fun to stop

I am tired and beat as I arrive home
But the price I was willing to pay
To visit with friends and have a great time
Has truly proven to be a wonderful day

I have something to eat and then go upstairs
To model my purchase of the day
It's a jumpsuit that looks more like a dress
And at only $16.95, quite a bargain I'd say

I'm grateful for friends who remember me
And we plan to meet again soon
I remember them all in my prayers
And can't wait until the next time in June

April 18th

It is Sunday morning and I'm tired again
Which comes as no surprise to me
But I remain cheerful and go out again
To purchase that special tee

I come home to rest and sleep for a while
For tonight we have special plans
Wilbur has gotten us tickets to see
The Manhattan Transfer again

It is a great show and we're home by ten
And it's up the stairs to bed we go
I am restless and sleep does not come
I am reliving the entire show

My legs are restless and I jerk and pull
Poor Wilbur suffers the blows
I am not able to control my legs
And so to the guestroom he goes

Sleep finally comes after taking some meds
To quiet my legs and the pain
This is not uncommon with Fibromyalgia
But I hate going through this again

I am thankful for having two days in a row
With fun and excitement for me
I pray that I will continue to heal
But I'm worried about good day number three

April 19th

It is Monday morning and I cannot move
My entire body is in pain
I stay in bed for quite a long time
And then I phone the doctor again

I explain my activities over the past few days
And he listens very carefully to me
I tell him I take three steps forward and two steps backward
And he says that's the way it will be

I don't like the verdict but believe that it's true
I haven't built enough strength yet
He encourages me to keep up the pace
And remember to know when to rest

He implies that I expect too much from myself
And that I must surely recognize
That Fibromyalgia and Osteoporosis
Are tough for a person of my size

I acknowledge this fact reluctantly
And know that he is very wise indeed
But I still want to move in fast forward
And live my life as I please

I rest for the day and hope for the best
That tomorrow will bring some relief
For now I need a good night's sleep
And I pray for I truly believe

April 20th

I am grateful to wake up feeling rested
And fuel my body each and every cell
I promise to take it easy today
I have class tonight and want to do well

I declined the offer to hike every Monday
I think that would be pushing too far
Although there's nothing better I'd like
It would be foolish of me to raise the bar

I'm doing enough at this stage in my life
And know that recovery is slow
I've always been so active before
That this comes as a really big blow

I'm very aware of more serious things
And have friends who are dealing with more
So I am truly humbled and touched to know
That I can still live my life slowly but sure

April 21st

This day began quite softly I'd say
Laying quietly in the bed
Safe and warm and toasty indeed
As I begin to plan in my head

The errands to run that will take time
And I want to be able to do them all
I have a truly wonderful breakfast
And run through how the day will unfold

It's off to the bank to grab some cash
And do some shopping in town
Then off for my visit to the therapist
And back to the pharmacy I'm bound

I love turning on the computer each day
For the message that greets me every time
It says, "I love you Grammy" in red
And was written by Kendra so kind

Wilbur worked out in the yard today
And when I returned back home
A big bunch of daffodils greeted me
On the table all yellow and in full bloom

Last night's class was wonderful
Although I'm a little bit sore
I know that I'm building up my strength
And want to continue for sure

The days are brighter and so am I
The weather finally feels like spring
I feel that I could actually turn cartwheels
My heart is lighter and so I sing

There really is joy in everything
If we only take the time to see
I'm beginning to feel less like doom
And more like the freedom to be me

April 22nd

Today was a wonderful surprise indeed
A day I did not quite expect
Alayne was unusually pleasant to me
And the boys always treat me with respect

We drove to a place called "Magic Wings"
A butterfly conservatory and gardens
We stopped and had a delicious lunch
And then toured the beautiful grounds

The butterflies were from all over the world
And quite spectacular in color
The gardens reminded me of my days in Florida
It was filled with wonder and splendor

We chatted with ease no tension was present
And I was truly grateful for the fact
Because there is usually a moment or two
When I am criticized for this or that

We drove home in Alayne's new car
And spoke mostly about soccer and play
That is the game that engages the boys
We totally enjoyed the entire day

I came home to rest up for a bit
And had a small bite to eat
Then it was time for aerobics class
And I felt energized without defeat

I am most grateful and blessed indeed
To have had such a wonderful day
I'm looking forward to more of them
And I'll remember to say thank you when I pray

April 23rd

It is gloomy, rainy and cold today
It is Fosamax day once again
I am even more grateful for yesterday
I am surprised that there is little pain

It's almost time for breakfast now
I've waited the allotted time limit
I'm ready to eat something really good
And plan to have a big bowl of grits

I'm doing two loads of laundry today
And after that I will pack for two days
For later today Wilbur will drive me to Amy's
And tomorrow we're headed off to see Kendra play

We're going to Providence for an overnight stay
To watch her team on Saturday and Sunday
There will be four basketball games in total to see
And I'm looking forward to getting away

It means that I'm making progress you see
For this is something I would not consider before
But now I am gaining more strength every day
Hooray, I can finally plan to be outdoors

April 24th

The day started out very cheery and bright
We had breakfast and packed up the car
We drove to Providence Rhode Island
Which proved to be not all that far

We watched the first game it was most exciting
But did not turn out to be a win
And between games we took Olivia outside
That's when the trouble began

She played in the playground with her mother
And then she began to run too fast
Out into the crowded parking lot
I ran after her and took quite a blast

I fell on my face and broke two teeth
And scraped both my knees bloody and bruised
Amy freaked out and grabbed Olivia
And then came back to my rescue

My lip was cut and bleeding a lot
I rinsed it with water to clean the debris
A parking lot does not have much give
And I just lay there until I could see

All in all the damage was not too great
It could have been so much worse
A two-year-old running cannot be caught
I realize I am bleeding, sore and hurt

I get myself cleaned up the best that I can
And we go inside to watch the next game
They lose again and are disappointed once more
They are clearly not playing as a team

We decide to have dinner inside the hotel
I am much too tired to venture out
I order soft crab cakes and a glass of wine
Amy yells and Kendra pouts

April 25th

The day begins slowly and I take my shower
While Amy and the girls head down to the pool
I look in the mirror and see black and blues
I really look quite like a fool

We check out of the hotel and head off for brunch
We are all tired and hungry
I've paid for the hotel, dinner and brunch
And I'm feeling a little bit angry

Amy has asked to borrow some money
She is four hundred seventy dollars short
I've already spent way too much already
And I'm not sure how to give her support

I remain strong and resilient throughout the day
Although I really am in need of a doctor
But I refuse to let my Kendra down
So we head off for the two games to follow

We leave for home at around eight thirty
And arrive in Middletown by ten
Wilbur is there to pick me up
And I wait to let go until then

We get home by eleven and head off to bed
But I get up and take a hot shower
I need to release all the tension inside
I crawl into bed and start to sob

April 26th

I sleep in late while Wilbur calls the dentist
They tell him they can see me at three
He then calls the doctor to report the news
She listens but doesn't need to see me

I am frightened and scared to see the dentist
My body is rigid and in great pain
My lip is so swollen that all they can do
Is check the teeth and I must go back again

Wilbur phones Alayne out of courtesy
To let her know what has happened to me
I ask her not to be mad at her sister
It was not anyone's fault you see

She is quite alarmed and wants to know
Why I was doing the chasing
I tell her I was closest to Olivia
And that was my immediate reaction

I return to bed it's been quite a day
The dentist thinks I had a concussion
It doesn't really matter at all
I am too tired to have the discussion

Wilbur holds me close and lets me cry out
And tell him all about the weekend
The things that I saw and did not like
Between Amy, Olivia and Kendra

Amy calls to see how I am doing
I tell her I have called her sister
She doesn't like that and tells me she's hurt
And hangs up on me leaving me to blister

April 27th

No one calls to see how I am
And then Kathy shows up with flowers
I empty my heart and she listens with tears
And tells me things will be better tomorrow

I go back to bed and wait for Wilbur to come home
He is working away all day long
He arrives to see me crying again
He tucks me in and keeps me warm

We talk about how ungrateful children can be
We both know that this is the case
The girls are fighting amongst themselves
And I think my condition should come first

I go to bed angry and hurt once more
I'm still swollen, bruised and in pain
But the girls are too busy nursing their hurt
To care or to give a damn

I am so disappointed in both of them
I am unable to release my cares
The feelings I'm having are just too great
I look to heaven and seek comfort there

April 28th

I sleep in late again what else is new?
I need to rest more now than ever
This time I feel like I've taken two steps forward
And ten steps backward forever

The sun is shining but it is cold outside
So I try to stay warm inside the house
I finally call Alayne to ask her if
She has heard from her sister the mouse?

She tells he that she has and it was not pleasant
That Amy wanted to pick a big fight
I'm sorry to hear that the news is not good
And we talk for awhile into the night

I have an idea and phone my ex-spouse
His wife Rita answers the phone
I ask if Alan is available to speak
She tells me he is not at home

But she promises to call him on his cell
And have him return my call
I explain that Amy is in financial need
And I cannot cover it all

He says he will call me tomorrow at home
To let me know his financial condition
I know that he is certainly not cash rich
But I think it's time he knows the true situation

I speak with Rita, his wife again
And she tells me she thinks of me often
And gives me credit for living with him
As long as I did, she is ready for a coffin

We talk for some time and I thank her again
For keeping Alan safe and grounded
She says they're having a difficult time
I promise her prayers for all unbounded

April 29th

I get up early for I cannot sleep
Amy called me late last night
She cried and told me how hurt she was
I could not endure the fight

So I told her we would talk some other time
When I was a bit stronger than now
She didn't like my response at all
But I must take care of myself first somehow

The day is sunny but still a bit cold
I have a few errands to run
For tomorrow we leave for Pennsylvania
To tour Longwood Gardens what fun

I want to go badly and not disappoint Wilbur
It's his birthday and besides the good weather
We will meet up with Cory his daughter we love
And spend the entire weekend together

I'm going to pack my suitcase soon
So that I have everything I need
Clothing, books, meds and shoes
I just hope I have the strength to succeed

I'm doing everything I can to protect myself
I want this weekend to go well
I truly need to have an enjoyable time
The last weekend was really hell

April 30th

I am excited about our trip today
I have packed everything we need
I fail to anticipate my tiredness
And I have mixed emotions as we leave

The drive is approximately five hours long
I am quite comfortable in the car
We arrive around one o'clock
I am happy to have traveled this far

Cory is there to greet us with smiles
We are delighted to see her as well
We unpack and then head off to lunch
At the Simon Pierce glass factory she loves so well

Our lunch is superb and we stay for a while
To spend some time in the shop
She has already been there to purchase a vase
When we look things are pricey so we stop

We head back to the inn and I take a nap
While Cory and Wilbur play cribbage
Then we make an agreeable plan
On where to go for dinner

We pick a place called Vicker's Tavern
Thinking the cost will not send us over the limit
The food is delicious and very expensive
And we enjoy every morsel and tidbit

We return to the inn to end the night
We are tired from the day's events
I head off to sleep before everyone else
For I am totally spent

May 1st

Today is the day we've previously chosen
To tour the famous Longwood Gardens
It is truly an entire day's long event
To see everything and film the gardens

Cory is amazed at the expanse of it all
Over one thousand acres and conservations
There are over six hundred employees in total
To maintain the grounds and provide tours

We happen to be there on Arbor Day
And there are lots of special events taking place
We try to catch the Bell Tower Concert
There is so much time and space

We rest for a while and grab some lunch
For our legs are tired and sore
But we continue on with the tour of the grounds
We want to see everything that's for sure

We head back to the Inn where we all take a rest
And make reservations to have dinner at the inn
We are delightfully surprised with our meals
They are even better than the previous dinner had been

We take a little walk in the cool night air
Which smells of lilacs and jasmine
This is really a spectacular place
Where Spring is fully in swing

We say good night and agree to meet
In the morning to have a good breakfast
This has been a most enjoyable visit
And I want it to last and last

May 2nd

We meet each other at the allotted time
And pick a diner for breakfast
We enjoy our meal and take our time
We know it will be our last

At least for awhile for we do not visit
As Cory lives in Salt Lake City
It is a very long distance away
And we'd love to be more able to see her

We drive back to the Inn for it's checkout time
And we want to stay close and hug forever
But it's time to take off for the long drive home
And Cory to catch her plane home to Utah

We arrive home at four and there are messages waiting
We unpack and then answer the calls
My brother tells me the result of the MRI
The news is not good at all

There is a growth on his spine
About four centimeters long
They will do a biopsy using a scan
And hopefully find out what is wrong

I'm feeling so sad because I'd believed all along
That the bone problem would pass from mother to me
How can it be possible for it to affect my brother?
Oh my God, I wish it were me

I speak to Alayne and give her the news
And ask her to specifically pray
The surgery is scheduled for next Monday
And I will have to go there and stay

I am feeling too sad to even talk
But Wilbur holds me so close
He tries so hard to comfort me
But I am really feeling morose

May 3rd

Today is Wilbur's 56th birthday
And I am too tired to bake
I give him his presents and explain to him
That there will be no birthday cake

He is happy with his gifts and tells me that
I am his best gift of all time
I love him so much and am filled with tears
When will I accept that he is mine?

The mail comes and with it a few new cards
And a check from Alan to me
I hold on to it now for I do not know
If Amy will return my check to me

She says she is hurt and will not accept
Any financial assistance from me
She is truly unreasonable and out of control
When it comes to speaking with me

She has uttered some very nasty words
Which resulted in much hurt and sting
I don't know what it will take to get her on track
But it is not my business, responsibility or thing

She must come to her senses on her own
Or with the help of a counselor
I have made that very suggestion to her
But she would not listen to me before

I will pray for her and her family
In a very special way tonight
To ask God to heal her and help her to see
We are her support and not to run in fright

May 4th

Today does not begin well at all
We spent the night in the Emergency Room
It seems like there was more damage done
When last weekend I took the famous fall down

We addressed the bruises and bleeding at once
And overlooked the pain in my chest
That turned out to be a big mistake
There's a contusion on the wall of my chest

They x-rayed my lungs, chest and ribs
To be sure there was nothing broken
The staff was very accommodating to us
Even though there were very few words spoken

I'm glad it was not a heart attack
The pain was so sharp and deep
That we both became quite afraid
When the doctor suggested that I be seen

I'm angry and hurt and need some time
To cool off before I phone my children
For this will surely fuel Amy's anger
And she is already guilt ridden

My brother's condition has me worried to death
When will we all catch a much-needed break?
I am stressed to the point that I am afraid
Of just how much more I can take

I'll try to stay calm and rest for the day
Reading and watching some TV
I know that I do not feel well at all
Please God I want to feel more like me

This chronic pain is awful at best
And I am aware of my blessings
I'll try to be quiet and not make a fuss
And claim this as another of life's lessons

May 5th

Today is the day I see the therapist
And since I am not able to drive
I've asked Wilbur to accompany me
And share the session along with the ride

I hope that this is all right with Diane
I cannot imagine that she will object
In fact I'm counting on Wilbur to remember
The parts that I'm likely to forget

Just how long does recovery actually take?
Or will this go on forever?
I was beginning to feel a bit stronger
But now I question if I'll ever be better

I truly want to get past this setback
And know in my mind this will pass
It has taken seven months already
And I want the healing to go fast

I'm following the directions so clearly given
By the doctors who are in charge
I am once again reminded of the fact
That I'm not the one in control; it is God

Please help me to learn and truly see
The greater picture at large
And remember to count all of my blessings
Sixty plus years of them, thank you God

May 6th

Yesterday's session was quite a trip
Diane thinks that I'm very depressed
I'm not sure that I agree with her
I think I need a well-deserved rest

It's off to see Doc Spiegel today
I'm curious to hear what he has to say
The pain in my chest is still quite severe
And I'd like to have it end today

Then it's off for a quick trim for my hair
That should not take very long
And then we go see the dentist again
To see if he can fix what is wrong

All in all this fall has caused me much grief
Both physical and emotional too
I received a note from Amy that said
She was sorry for all I've been through

Somehow it did not comfort me much
It seemed to be more defensive
I've read it three times and still it seems
She's really giving me more of her nonsense

I'm still worried to death about Uncle Bert
The signs all point to bone cancer
I could not take losing him to that disease
Losing mother that way was a disaster

May 7th

Yesterday's dentist visit went just fine
He aligned up my two front teeth and then
Joked with me a little about the fall
And told me how lucky I was again

Then it was off to see Doctor O
She is truly a great doctor and genius
She immediately put me on Prednisone
And said I would soon find relief

Of course she is right, the sac around my heart
Had swollen to protect my life
And in so doing put pressure on the chest wall
Causing me all of the pain and strife

Then back to the pharmacy I go
A bit deflated once again
I want this insidious pain to stop
And to never return again

I return home to rest and take my pills
This is beginning to be quite an annoyance
I want to feel good about myself
Relaxed, clear thinking and buoyant

Perhaps tomorrow after the MRI
I'll get a chance to be still
That it was on the top of my list
To be quiet, listen and be still

May 8th

It is off to New Milford we drive today
So early in the morning to begin
I have taken my pill to relax my body
For this MRI testing I want to win

They get me set up inside the machine
And have to pad the shoulder blocks
Because I am too narrow across
And they want the film to be clear and locked

They give me earplugs to soften the noise
It helps to keep me quite silent
I; however, take this opportunity
To pray and meditate in quiet

The test is about one-half hour long
I'm happy to be done with it
I thank the staff for their patience with me
They all agree I was quite a hit

I did not move and that made it easy
For the filming to take place on time
The pill has now made me so relaxed
It feels like I've had a glass of wine

We stop along at the hardware store
Where Wilbur buys a new wheelbarrow
To replace the one that was stolen last year
Perhaps he'll give me a ride tomorrow

May 9th

Today is Mother's Day and I feel exhausted
I choose to forgo the party at Wilbur's sister's
Wilbur presents me with a lovely gift and card
And I choose to stay home but will miss her

I know he is hesitant to leave me alone
But three hours in the car is too much
Not to mention the people and the crowd
I know this will be very tough

I send him along to pick up his mother
And take her along to his sister's house
There is a lot of family attending today
And I feel a little like a coward mouse

But I know in my heart that I've done the right thing
To be home alone and be still
I rest on the couch and watch some TV
And allow myself to do just as I will

All in all it turns out to be a restful day
With me thinking about my dear mother
I've sent Wilbur along with gifts to bring
To his wonderful and loving mother

I must admit I enjoyed the quiet time
Instead of the hustle and bustle
That usually goes along with a picnic so fine
And I finally relax with no trouble

Thank you God for this day alone
I have thought and prayed a lot
I realize that I can no longer be
Like "Johnny on the spot"

May 10th

Today is the day my brother goes to the hospital
They will biopsy the growth on his spine
I know he is terrified and so am I
I wish I could be there by his side

But our good friend Arlene is there for him
To keep him from being alone
I know how scary this procedure is
They are looking for cancer on the bone

I almost feel guilty as if I was the one
Who expected to have this dreaded disease
It was the cause of our mother's death
And I have all the symptoms with ease

I pray for my brother and the doctor too
I know this will not be easy for him
They will cut and probe with cameras inside
And then remove a good size shim

I wait for his call when they release him home
It comes and he is in great pain
I try to stay uplifted while I speak to him
But I resort to crying once again

I assure him that we will work things out
No matter whatever the cost
After all he is my only sibling
And we do love each other the most

I want to see him for myself
But know I must wait until Wednesday
For tomorrow it's off to see Doctor O again
So she can check on my progress I pray

I phone the girls to let them know
That the procedure has been completed
But there are no results yet and furthermore
There are many more tests yet to be scheduled

May 11th

I wake up and pray and then pray some more
I want to know how Bert is feeling
I finally pick up the phone and call him
He says the pain has him reeling

I'm so far away just 50 + miles
But it might as well be cross-country
Because I'm not yet strong enough
To drive there and make the journey

I go to my appointment with Doctor O
She is so delightful and charming
My progress is great she tells me at last
But remembers to issue her warning

No activities for at least two more weeks
The chest wall is still in need of more healing
The Prednisone has helped reduce the swelling
I must remain calm; not quite the way I am feeling

I promise to abide by her words of truth
But I'm no longer out of her sight
When I begin to plan my visit to my brother
I must see for myself with my own eyes

Wilbur is leery of me taking the long drive
I assure him that I'm up to the task
So I go to bed early and get good sleep
So that I can awake feeling very relaxed

May 12th

The day is here and I arise very early
I am excited to make the trip
We sent some flowers yesterday
To Arlene who has been such a big help

I get on the road at about 9:15
And drive my way directly to his house
I find my brother much better than I thought
And he wants to go out for some lunch

I'm more than delighted to accommodate him
But I see the pain in his eyes
He is hiding from me his little sister
But I am on to him and we both cry

He admits he is scared of what is next
In the arsenal of tests to come
I know the bone scan will tell for sure
If there is cancer inside of his bones

The growth on the outside has been biopsied
But we both think it will be removed
He is scared to death and I pray for him
His concern has touched me and I am moved

He is concerned about the distance between us
I assure him we will work it all out
We can always sell the house in Manchester
And build onto our big old farmhouse

I get him home and back into bed
He is tired from the trip outside
But he has eaten a good hearty lunch
And I got to be seated at his side

I begin the drive home and run into traffic
I've not dealt with in quite a long time
But I use the time to reflect and pray
That soon this mess we will leave far behind

May 13th

When I arrived home yesterday
I was quite exhausted and worried
I spoke with Wilbur about my concerns
He assured me and not to be hurried

We have plenty of land on which to build
An addition for dear Uncle Bert
No matter what happens he will not allow
My brother or me to be hurt

This man is a wonderful partner for life
The very thing I thought I would never find
But amidst the messes and traumas that happen
He is happily there and ever so kind

I am grateful and loved and thankful for all
The blessings, which have been bestowed
Although some of them come in disguise
I now recognize what is true love

I am free to be me however that is
Like a butterfly floating on air
I think I'm beginning to learn and accept
That life is for living and not despair

I am humbled beyond the words I can use
I know that I don't have to perform
I am loved simply because of whom I am
How can I possibly go wrong?

Thank you God for the chance to serve
And spend some time with my brother
The dying words from our mother's mouth
Were "be sure to take care of each other"

May 14th

Today I awoke almost excited
The news was really quite sad
But to matter what happens next
It will not turn out too bad

The growth Bert has is malignant
He goes to see a specialist next week
We do not yet know what they will do
But we know we will deal with this for keeps

His mind is sharp and he wants to live
In fact we are designing a plan
To sell the house in Manchester
And bring him home to our land

I speak with the therapist at length today
And bring her the gift of song
She thanks me for the music and words
And says that I am very strong

An addition to the house with full privacy
Seems to be the next order in line
Wilbur has begun to draw the plans
Now we just need money and time

We're going to Alayne's house tonight
To celebrate Graham's 9th birthday
A very happy occasion indeed
And a bright happy young boy I'd say

Thank you God for Your gifts today
And all the others before
Please watch over us all and keep us safe
We'll have many petitions more

May 15th

We awake very early again today
Wilbur is going out fishing
I am up and ready to go
It seems like I have a new mission

I know I need a purpose to live
And I've not quite understood in the past
I now know that I've been in training
To take on this brand new task

It doesn't really feel like a task at all
It seems more like a true blessing
If Bert can make it through the next few months
He'll have a new reason for living

He has worked seven days a week for 10 years
And it is time now that he got some real rest
We will be delighted to build the addition for him
And give him everything, our very best

He loves it out here in the country
With no city traffic involved
He can putter around in his own little space
And also around in the yard

We've spoken of our love for each other
Which is quite a surprise to hear
It's delightful that he trusts Wilbur and me
Because we both love him so dear

May 16th

It is Sunday and I am up early again
Excited and pleased with myself at last
Yesterday Kathy and I took a 6-mile walk
And yes I was glad to be up to the task

My right heel is sore but nothing else
I am truly grateful for that
There are no other problems to report
I think I'll take that pat on my back!

My energy level is being fueled again
With vitamins and very good food
My appetite has happily returned to me
And Wilbur is also feeling good

I speak with my brother—he is quite scared
Of what lies ahead for him
But together we will make it through this scare
And look forward to the future again

I wrote a letter to John and Lynn
And received an instant reply
John was just going to e-mail me
When his computer beeped "here am I"

It is truly amazing the way God works
If only we pay some attention
I know for myself that I'm ready to receive
And act upon any intention

May 17th

It is Monday morning and I sleep in late
I need some strength for tomorrow
I'm going with Bert to the Urologist
To take notes and be there for what follows

I phone Doc Spiegel and Dr. Oltikar too
To obtain the names of some other Doctors
Bert should at least have another opinion
Before he submits to any other procedures

He is happy I'm coming and I'm glad also
I want to be there for his support
Encouragement is what he needs most right now
Along with some prayers and a good report

My right hip is telling me that I pushed too far
But not giving me too much pain
Just a little reminder to take care of myself
So my strength I can continue to regain

I clean out some drawers to clear the mess
That has been stuffed away since last October
It is like a purification act in some way
Like getting rid of the cobwebs left over

Wilbur is painting the porch outside
Getting the house ready for summer
Spring has finally arrived at long last
And has lifted my spirits so somber

Thank you for my blessings today
And the lessons I've learned thus far
Please keep me open to receive Your words
And continue to look toward the stars

May 18th

The day began extremely early with Wilbur off to work
And me traveling the long way to pick up Uncle Bert

For it's off to the specialist for his expert opinion
Of what the next step is and how it should be taken

I assist my brother with the paperwork that seems to be endless to him
But I remain calm and take over the task and encourage him to relax every limb

The news is encouraging but more tests must be run
They are already scheduled by Friday they will all be done

He prescribes a new drug, an Anti-Cancer drug indeed
We head to the pharmacy with an all out speed

Thank goodness his insurance covers the cost of the meds
$565.00 dollars in all would be over our heads

We have a good lunch with our dear friend Arlene
And then I bring him home because he is in great pain

I leave him now to begin the drive home and count the blessings for the day
We have a lot to look forward to and I am filled with love all the way

Thank God for the strength to stand by his side and to be able to tell
The love and respect we share with each other and the many blessings as well

May 19th

I am weary and tired from yesterday
So I take extra time in the bed
Before I am able to get up and move
And arouse my sleepy little head

I smell the coffee it is simply divine
And I take my time down the stairs
I'm enjoying the sense of feeling so well
And take the time to breathe in the fresh air

Wilbur is pleased that I'm sunny and bright
My heart is filled to the brim
I tell him I must let out some of the love
And the feelings that I have for him

I'm reminded again through a little pain
To not push myself too far
So today I will rest and write my lines
Staying within my limits, which is hard

There are so many things I want to get done
But I respect my body and spirit
I'm finally learning and adhering to
My situation and its set limits

I realize that I will never be pain free
And that I must move about with caution
I accept this fact and know this to be true
I am blessed beyond my fair portion

May 20th

Today begins slowly, no hurry in mind
We have breakfast and coffee together
We are headed off to Manchester again
To assess the house at my brother's

We drive along very happily
With the sun shining down upon us
I am struck by the feeling I have inside
That we are being filled with great goodness

We arrive and are greeted by Bert at the door
He is so very pleased to see us
We take paper and pencil and begin to make lists
Of what to fix up and what to get rid of

Then we make drawings of his furniture
To try and plan out his new space
This is going to be a daunting task at best
But we are filled with the sense of God's grace

We stop at the hospital to pick up some meds
Which Bert will take for tomorrow's tests
He will have a busy day to say the least
And he begs me to stay at home and rest

I agree once I know that he will get rides
For the many trips he must make
Back and forth to the hospital for multiple scans
And then back home for a much needed break

We go up to the choir loft—this is his second home
For twenty years now to him so dear
He packs up his music and plays a tune
And we all leave shedding a few tears

We know this part is difficult for him
Because it has been his whole life
But now we begin another phase for us
Together we face this great fight

May 21st

I'm glad to be home and take the time
For strength and for myself
I remember that I must mind my needs
To continue to regain my health

I do a few loads of laundry and then
Go up to Wilbur's office to tell him
How much I love the life that we have
And how wonderful he is as my man

I then phone the rectory to speak with Carole
And thank her and tell her she is special indeed
She has become my brother's close friend
The one he shares with in times of need

She thinks this is lovely, thanks me for the call
I am truly grateful and blessed
For she is there when I cannot be
And I know she's a friend to trust

I will go tomorrow to meet the realtor
And discuss what the selling price should be
Bert is anxious to unload the burden
And on this point we all agree

How lucky are we to have the chance
To provide a place for Bert to live
Not merely exist but to have purpose and fun
I can think of no better gift

He is truly gifted and talented too
With music and a perfect ear
But I love him really for who he is
My brother so sweet and dear

May 22nd

Wilbur is up early to work at Camp Mohawk
It is a work-day for all the directors
Fixing and repairing what needs to be done
He is happy to be present and a worker

I get up fairly early myself
To make the drive to my brother's
To meet with the realtor and set a price
Hopefully some family will make an offer

We decide there are too many things to fix
And make arrangements to tackle a few
But we list the property in "as in" condition
And look to the future with a hopeful view

I do some yard work before I leave
And take Bert to the grocery store
That is a big laugh between us both
Because I never do the shopping anymore

He is greeted by all the employees he knows
And everyone asks how he is getting along
I am honored to meet the many folks
Who love him and make him feel he belongs

Then it is back home for Bert and some rest
And me to drive the long way home
Wilbur and I arrive at the same time
We are both exhausted to the bone

We celebrate our 7 ½ years together
And enjoy a glass or two of wine
We really are a true partnership
We recognize what we have is sublime

May 23rd

It is Sunday morning and I'm in some pain
Probably from yesterday's work in the yard
It is not too severe and serves as a reminder
Of the limits I must observe, which is hard

Bert's friend Sandy is driving him out
To have lunch with us later today
I know he wants to go to the nursery
Where he really feels free to play

We purchase some rosebushes to replace those
Which were lost in last winter's weather
Sandy and Bert each purchase one for us
What a wonderful and kind gesture

We look to Bert to advise on which roses
Are hearty, sturdy and will survive
He gives us his guidance and we pick the rest
With great hopes of keeping them alive

Wilbur cooks pork chops on the grill
They are juicy and tasty indeed
He makes a stir-fry of vegetables
And mixes them with pasta to please

Wilbur also bakes a fresh fruit pie
Which is gobbled up quickly before our eyes
I've never seen Bert eat sweets before
And we're pleased to see this new surprise!

May 24th

It is Monday and I am tired again
I'm thinking of the things to be done
Just cleaning out the Manchester house
Will take an army of friends to come

Bert has already arranged for the day
When the volunteers will arrive
I will be there to assist of course
But it will seem like a huge nose-dive

There are so many decisions to be made
Of what to keep or throw out
And then the things to sell at a tag-sale
It is too much for me to think about

I spend most of the day lost in a book
Which takes my mind somewhere steady
I forget that we are taking Granny to dinner
And I must rush around just to get ready

We drive to Madison 1 ½ hours away
And pick up Granny to take her out for a while
We have a most enjoyable meal all together
And then begin the trip home—oh the miles

We arrive home quite late and tired as well
I have trouble being in the car
Little outings are not too bad for me
But long drives push me way too far

We're happy and tired as we crawl into bed
We watch some TV and read
We talk for a little and clear our heads
We are present to each other indeed

Thank God for our blessings and the chance to see
Granny so cheerful and excited
She asked us to draw out our plans to expand
She seems to be genuinely delighted

May 25th

Today begins early; I'm not able to sleep
So I get up, have coffee and read
I fall back to sleep quite easily now
It seems sleep is what I really need

Tonight is my first time back at aerobics
And I'm both excited and nervous
I want to regain the strength that I've lost
And know it will take time and patience

It's a sunny day and not too cool
Yesterday was almost too cold
It is pleasant to look outside at the sun
Perhaps I'll go out and be bold

There are several errands that I could run
But I'm saving my energy for tonight
I want the experience to be a success
And I don't want to look like a fright

I know it will feel good to move my body
And be with friends who care
They've been calling and writing notes to me
With word of encouragement to share

How fortunate am I to have good friends
Who take the time to express
Their concern for me and for my health
To me this is just the best

May 26th

Today is my meeting with the therapist
At 9:30 so early in the morning
We talk for over an hour this time
I'm making good progress and I want to sing

But still I am deeply concerned about my brother Bert
And again I am not sleeping too well
There are so many things crowding my mind
I am unable to concentrate and be still

I drive out to Manchester to visit with Bert
I take him to the grocery store to shop
For a few things he needs to fuel his body
When I head home I'm ready to drop

I catch myself falling asleep at the wheel
At least six times I'm overcome
I know that I should pull over to rest
But I just simply want to get home

Finally a cop who has been following me
Pulls me over to see if I'm all right
I breakdown in tears and tell him I'm tired
He arranges for me to get a ride safely tonight

It is good to know that there are decent cops
Looking out for everybody's welfare
I realize he probably saved my life
And who knows what else I dare

May 27th

It is Thursday and I'm long overdue
For a haircut and color to boot
So it's off to see Doug whom I dearly love
He is always such a great hoot

I show him a picture of what I'd like
We agree to go quite a bit shorter
He colors and cuts my mop of hair
And says I look like my daughter

He teases me about how thick my hair is
And says he needs to use hedge clippers
I laugh and remind him how good it is
To sit in his chair as he chatters

I go home and rest for aerobics tonight
I am anxious to keep up my spirit
Everyone loves my new haircut
And tell me I look like a little kid

That's good enough for me to hear
And I coast my way through the class
I'm enjoying the movement of my body
And feel I'm getting stronger at last

May 28th

It is the beginning of the long holiday weekend
And we have made plans to go out tonight
With Lynne and Dave for dinner and dancing
To hear Nick and Nancy make music a delight

We meet lots of our friends who are also out
And catch up on all the good news
Until I share the news of my brother
Which has already given me the blues

We stay for a while but not too long
For Wilbur can see that I'm tired
We head off for home a little early
And to our soft bed we retire

Thank you God for all our good friends
Who help us travel along this way
We are so very blessed to have these folks
I remember them all as I pray

May 29th

Wilbur is out working in the yard today
There are so many things to do
I wish I had the energy to help
But I know what I'm not able to do

I rest for the day; we have plans for tonight
It is our monthly evening of Trivia
We bring dessert and the food is great
And we begin the evening together

But I have consumed many glasses of wine
And fall asleep at the table
Wilbur picks me up and brings me home
He is angry with me—I have failed him

I have failed myself and I feel like a fool
I knew it from the very start
I brought tonic to drink and somehow I allowed
Myself to get stuck—not too smart

I'm trying to kill the awful pain
Both physical and emotional
But I know that this is not the right way
And I cannot forgive myself at all

Please help me God to do the right thing
When I am afraid and scared
I know I need to focus much better
And spend much more time in prayer

May 30th

The only good thing is that I sleep
Long into the morning
I apologize to Wilbur and then I call
The others to express that I'm sorry

There is silence between us the entire day
I wonder how long this will last
I am sad and angry with myself for this
Has happened to me in the past

Wilbur works outside again all day
He avoids speaking to me at all
I can't say that I blame him too much
I don't want to speak to anyone at all

Instead I busy myself with laundry
And change the sheets on the bed
I try to make something useful of myself
But I fall way short in my head

We sleep in silence and I am afraid
I don't have as much faith as Wilbur
Our relationship is really a partnership
But I don't feel as though I'm in the picture

I pray that I'm able to forgive myself
And that we can move forward from here
I need to take better care of myself
On that note I am very clear

May 31st

It's Memorial Day and I remember our dads
Who both spent time serving our country
Then we have our coffee and breakfast
And head off once again to meet Amy

We are going to Manchester to clean out some things
That Amy would like for her house
A dining room table and four chairs to match
And for the family room, an old weathered couch

She is held up, calls to say she'll be late
So I busy myself with some cleaning
The inspector is coming by tomorrow
To advise the buyers what is needed

Amy eventually shows up at the door
We see that she is angry and upset
We load up the van and away they go
Her attitude stinks, but I stay quiet you bet

We take Bert to the store for he needs more food
It is crowded and he is in great pain
We hurry through the many isles because
I want to see him get home and rest again

We drive home quietly to our little home
Where I feel safe and secure
I am beat by all the traveling
I just want to relax for sure

Amy phones later to thank us again
She seems to be in a much better mood
She has found a new cover for the couch
And Kendra has polished all of the wood

I'm happy she has these things for her house
It has not been easy for her and the girls
I'm surprised that Carlos is there to assist
Perhaps there is hope for their marriage still

June 1st

June is finally here at long last
But it is only 59 degrees outside
Wherever is that promised warm weather?
We are all of us staying inside

I got up quite early with much on my mind
Bills to pay and a trip to the bank
I had some coffee and a breakfast of grits
To fuel my tummy's empty tank

I ran the few errands and then came home
To catch up on last week's writing
Which proved to be quite humbling indeed
To put down those word into writing

I am brighter today and I truly thank God
For everyday is a new beginning
I always think that when I mess up
Someone is counting my sinning

I will drive later today to Manchester again
To spend the night with my brother
For we will go see the specialist again
At 9:30 in the morning

I want to know what the Doctor has in mind
As the next step in this endurance race
I think Bert should be on some strengthening pills
To help him win this fight and gain pace

I think Bert is not telling me everything
And I know that he is afraid
To be all alone and face this ordeal
Which is why we are assisting him and offering aid

Dear God please bless my brother with peace
And send some relief from his insidious pain
And also continue to bless Wilbur and me
With guidance for what we have planned

June 2nd

I did not drive to my brother's last night
The weather was too bleak and stormy
I went to aerobics class instead
And worked off my little tummy

Arlene has promised to give him a ride
To the Doctor's office and back
I'm really tired and nauseous today
So I'm glad to be able to hold back

We rented a dumpster for two weeks time
It should arrive this Friday
And with the help of the music group and friends
It should be filled up in its entirety

The task of cleaning and packing Bert's things
Seems to me to be quite a beast
To know what to keep and what to throw out
Will take two weeks time at the very least

I'm hoping he phones me with some good news
For the specialist is administering some shot
I'm not quite sure what it is intended to do
But I surely hope is helps the pain a lot

We are all anxious to begin the addition
But so far we have no official drawings
I'm hoping that Ed will come down soon
With something to take to Planning & Zoning

Please continue to bless us all as we try
To overcome this dreadful disease
And let me remember what my limits are
So I too can find some rest and relief

June 3rd

Yesterday afternoon was quite the sight
With hail pouring down from the skies
It looked like a snowstorm covering the ground
I could hardly believe my own eyes

My brother went to see the specialist yesterday
And received a shot in the abdomen
It was a cocktail of Zoladex & Chemotherapy
Then he goes back in three months again

I think that this is really good news
However I still remain anxious
If this doesn't work they will have to zap him
With radiation to shrink the cancer

He remains calm although I know it's a front
He puts on so that I don't worry
We can only hope and pray for him
But I want him to be well in a hurry

It is sunny and bright and clear today
And for this I'm truly grateful
For the weather has been really terrible
And today I seem a bit more cheerful

We are planning to have dinner out tonight
With business associates so dear
Whom we only seem to get together with
Once or twice during the entire year

So thank you God just once again
For the love of Wilbur and my brother
We are so fortunate to be able to express
Our love and concern for each other

June 4th

Last evening's dinner was such a treat
To be with people who care
We had a great meal and discussion too
Bob and Nancy are such a loving pair

Cynthia and Wilbur spoke together
We all shared what is going on in our lives
It proved to be so very interesting
To be free and to share our real ties

I was supposed to go with Wilbur today
To hear his presentation to the hospital
But I realized that I had already overdone
And so I remained home quiet and restful

I gardened and weeded a bit this afternoon
When the energy bunny finally hit me
It was such a pleasure to be outside
And take in the breezes so easily

We had a superb dinner, which Wilbur made
And we dined on an exquisite meal
And then took some time to spend together
In conversation that was truly real

Thank you God just once again
For a partner who cares so much
It seems to me to be such a miracle
To have someone to love and to trust

June 5th

Wilbur left early this morning at six
For his annual fishing trip
With good friends Jack and Roger in tow
To Maine they are headed for a week

They have been doing this trip for 20 years
And they so much look forward to it
They have such a great time being with each other
I am truly happy for them every bit

It gives me a chance to have time alone
For reflection, meditation and prayer
Or just relaxing and taking free time
To read a good book in my chair

I spend most of the day relaxing so that
Tomorrow we can travel to Manchester
To clean out the attic, garage and porch
And do some packing for my brother Bert

We have rented a Dumpster for two weeks time
With a group of ten to lighten the load
We look forward to being able to sort and throw out
But there will remain much more to unfold

I'm grateful for this time to be myself
And do or not do whatever comes to mind
To be free in thought and enjoy the house
And to thank everyone who has been so kind

I go to bed early to get some good sleep
To be ready for the next day we've planned
I know that it will be hard and difficult
But I know that we will form a band

A circle of love around "Uncle Bert"
To help him along the way
For he is only able to direct and sort
What will be kept or thrown away

June 6th

I drive early to Alayne's house this morning
The entire family has chosen to come
It is quite cool and dreary a day
And I'm grateful to just ride along

We arrive at 10:30 to begin the task
Of cleaning out closets so stuffed full
This seems at first quite easy to do
But Bert is a packrat, so we must sort through

Ethan and Graham are such a big help
Not to mention Alayne and Brian
The boys are able to crawl in the attic
They feel so helpful—it makes me cry

The rest of the gang shows up at noon
Ready for whatever is asked
It proves to be a daunting task at best
To clean up or toss in the trash

I am so grateful and thankful for friends
Who are willing to give up their day
For Bert alone would never be able to do
All that was accomplished today

I am tired and weak at the end of the day
And so I stay at my daughter's overnight
Ethan has given up his bed for me
And I am so thankful; I close my eyes tight

Sleep comes quite easily for me this time
I am worn out to say the least
But we all remain quite hopeful indeed
That Bert will conquer this ugly disease

June 7th

I awake after sleeping a full 9 hours
And come down to the smell of coffee
My daughter is so organized it seems
There is not a thing to do left for me

I pour myself a very large cup
And wait for the boys to come down
I sit with them while they eat their breakfast
And then Brian leaves for downtown

He kisses the boys, Alayne and me
And off to work he is headed for the day
I pack up my things and get ready to leave
I kiss and thank them all for yesterday

I drive home alone in silence this morning
I'm grateful and moved to tears
To think that I have not been so close
To these members of my family so dear

I realize that my body is in severe pain
From all the work done yesterday
I phone Doc Spiegel to get some pain meds
So that I can continue to help along the way

Alayne and I will travel again tomorrow
To help sort through the many boxes
The ones that were filled for Bert to go through
And help him sort through years of pictures and letters

Thank you dear God for the opportunity to serve
In whatever capacity You choose
For I have learned to treasure each day
As another chance to win and not lose

June 8th

I awake early to begin the long day
And drive to Alayne's house by nine
We head off to Manchester again
And find my brother in much pain

We sort through the boxes of pictures
And ask his help to let us know
The people who appear in all the pictures
That are members of our family so dear

We do not recognize many of them
But Bert is able to pick out
Some of the many identities
Thus we keep these and do not through them out

The day is quite emotional for me
As we uncover some very old letters
And watching my brother suffer in pain
Does nothing to make me feel better

Alayne is anxious to document the history
That is in the many boxes contained
So that at long last we will have some idea
Of who is who both family and friends

We drive home and I find myself in some pain
So I take meds and lie down to rest
I want so badly to attend aerobics tonight
To work off the pain and the stress

The class is successful and I feel good
Although tired to the very core
I soak in the tub for quite a long time
And feel better than I did before

Thank you again for another day
To be of service and use
It feels to me like I've been set free
From the threat of that ever present noose

June 9th

It is Wednesday morning and I awake early
To fuel my body with breakfast
I have a few errands to run
And I want to be up to the task

Yesterday I polished the bedroom set
That belonged to my parents so dear
They purchased in the year 1932
And I want to keep it and have it near

I'll go looking for an iron headboard today
So that it will fit in our guestroom
I'm anxious to have it and to replace
The mis-matched pieces that are in this room

We uncovered so many treasures so dear
The tin-types from 1865
It is going to take quite some time
To sort through all the surprises

I am grateful to have a daughter who cares
And wants to document the family history
Before my brother and I are both gone
She will scrapbook each and every picture

I am going to attend a meeting tonight
Of the Northwest Writers of Connecticut
There will be two guest speakers to enlighten us
On matters of writing and getting published

June 10th

Yesterday's pain was quite severe
So I focused on writing and reading
While running a few errands in between
Before attending the evening's meeting

The Northwest Writers of Connecticut
Met from seven o'clock to nine
The McGoldrick's were the guest speakers
And imparted much wisdom divine

They spoke about writing and publishing
And that you must obtain a real agent
Who is the right person to work with you
And give true insight to what is meant

I was happily surprised to find such diversity
Among the many folks in attendance
Some were writing fiction and novels
While others were documenting real events

There were a few who were writing non-fiction
Which is where my writing belongs
I came home encouraged and quite renewed
And so I continue along with these poems

Mrs. McGoldrick likened my writing
To that of Simple Abundance
Which is a book I refer to daily
For both inspiration and guidance

I feel truly blessed to have this chance
To express my thoughts in this way
In hope that it will inspire someone else
Who is living with chronic pain and is afraid

June 11th

Dear Cindy

The community at large is truly blessed
To have you to teach our class
Because of your dedication to us
We each push beyond our past

You inspire me to reach new heights
Which before seemed totally out of my realm
But you encourage body, mind and spirit
I am so grateful you are at the helm

When at first I joined the class
I thought I would leave in tears
But you have guided and instructed me
To reach way beyond my fears

Osteoporosis and Fibromyalgia
Are enough to deal with alone
But with the help of this aerobics class
I am feeling both better and strong

I have new purpose and am able to see
A new life ahead filled with hope
And to treasure each day that lies ahead
To be able to deal with and cope

So thank you again from me and from all
For your belief, inspiration and devotion
We each reap so many benefits
You are truly loved with every emotion

—Lois Pike

June 12th

Today I awake and relive yesterday's outing
Which turned out to be such a fun day
I went to Graham's class to help assist
With Pirate's Day and activities along the way

There were games to play and treasure hunts
And the children had so much fun
Alayne introduced me to all her friends
She is truly valued for all she has done

It was a side of her I had not seen before
It made me very proud of her indeed
She has done a great job with her two sons
And with everything that the school needs

I awake today in thanks and in pain
My rib cage is completely on fire
I move around slowly and take my meds
I must rest for I am very tired

I've been busy all week and am so surprised
To find myself in this situation again
I thought I had paced myself easily
And yet here once again is much pain

A reminder once more to stop and rest
I am not a smooth running machine
I so long to have this pain disappear
That is my prayer and my dream

But rest is the order of the day
The message to me is quite clear
For tonight Wilbur returns from his trip
And I am grateful for I love him so dear

I've been given this week to do as I please
And I think that I've handled it well
But it will be wonderful to have Wilbur home
To share with him the many stories to tell

June 13th

Wilbur arrived home early last evening
We had so many stories to share
We talked very late into the night
Our souls open to each other to bear

We get up this morning and have a bite to eat
Before heading off to Manchester again
There is still much work there to be done
But this time I'm still in a lot of pain

We drive along and talk for a while
I tell him about last week's work done
I expect most of the same folks to return
To complete most of the rest and then some

I find myself weepy and quite overcome
The work seems to loom large ahead
I stick to upstairs and packing some boxes
While Wilbur and Bert downstairs they head

They are cleaning out the furnace room
When some of the others arrive
They each pick a spot to begin their work
I can hardly believe my eyes

We order some pizza for the break
And sit down to eat for a few minutes
Then it's back to work and the task at hand
I am stunned when it is almost finished

We head back home after saying goodbye
And I am quiet and silently humming
I think of Bert all alone in the house
And I know he is afraid and lonely

We arrive home and I find that I'm totally spent
I soak for a while in the tub
I cry for a bit and then ask Wilbur
To come upstairs and give me a hug

June 14th

I sleep in late until eight o'clock
And get up to have some breakfast
I remember the toll of yesterday
And I vow to take today slowly at best

I remember my phone call to Kathy last night
When she told me my expectations are too high
This entire challenge is so overwhelming
I forget to take it one step at a time

I plan to lay low for most of the day
Catching up on some good books to read
And then talking to Bert on the phone
To find out how he really feels

I know yesterday was tough on him
He did not take enough time to rest
I should follow my own advice before
Giving it out to him to follow like a test

I'll be meeting with Diane later today
There is so much happening in my life
I hope I can remember it all
So she can offer me some good advice

Thank you God for another day
To spend with my brother so dear
Please help him along and ease his pain
And take away some of his fears

June 15th

Today begins early just once again
But I return to my bed so sweet
I realize that there is nothing to hurry for
And so I drift back off to sleep

I recall telling Diane yesterday
Of my inability to concentrate and focus
I told her I feel somewhat scattered
She says I can expect much more of this

There are so many changes happening everyday
It's a wonder I can think at all
I feel like a mere speck of dust
Hurdling through space with no control

I must remember my Dad's Serenity Prayer
And not try to change what I'm not able
And remember to be patient with myself
Which to me seems like turning the tables

I am grateful indeed for each new day
And the surprises that come along
Although there is much residual pain
I generally feel that I'm getting strong

I go to class feeling very excited
And find that I'm now able to do
Twenty pushups in a row
Now that's improvement I think, don't you?

I speak with Bert for a short time on the phone
Before heading up to the bath
Wilbur and Ed have made changes to the plans
And we are excited to see the final plan at last

June 16th

The closing is less than one month away
And already I'm getting nervous
We gave our final offer for credits
To the folks who are going to purchase

The appraiser will come later today
And walk through the house with our realtor
I trust that the figures will come out right
So we can move forward with nothing further to consider

I'm experiencing much pain in my ribcage today
It seems to come from out of nowhere
But I am learning to slow down at last
For my body to rest and repair

I'm going for a haircut this afternoon
With nothing else planned for the day
The laundry is done and the house picked up
I can simply read for the rest of the day

I take my meds to quiet the pain
But it still remains very present
I'm learning to listen more closely to what
My body tells me instead of my head

Peace and quiet are the order of the day
And I find that I must adhere to and respect
The limits, which have been placed on me
Even though I want to play and not rest

So thank you again for another day
When I know that I'm really alive
For pain is the sign to slow down and rest
If I truly want to survive

June 17th

Today I awake in much pain again
I am truly surprised of this fact
I rested my body and soul yesterday
And I think my strength should be back

And so I am relegated to rest some more
Another day to relax and read
But I'm none-the-less blessed because of this
I acknowledge what my body really needs

Wilbur is here to help with massage
And to release the nerve pain inside
My ribs are so sore; they are resistant to touch
I am fortunate Wilbur is here at my side

I cannot attend aerobics tonight
I am disappointed that I am unable
Cindy is upset that I am in so much pain
But I will return to class as soon as I'm able

Hopefully tomorrow we'll see my brother
As I've not seen him for almost a week
We talk on the phone almost every day
But he needs company with whom he can speak

Thank you dear God for this time to rest
Although it is clearly not my will
I know that You know what is best for me
And so I have learned to be still

June 18th

Today we travel to visit my brother
We pack up some kitchen things
There is still so much that needs to be done
We must wait to see what the future brings

We mark the boxes as pots and pans
And stack them up with the rest
If we can keep up packing at this pace
We should be finished in no time at best

We meet with Arlene and have lunch together
It is good for Bert to get out
He enjoys his lunch as we all do
It's great to see him out and about

There remain many things left to work out
With the buyers who are making things harder
They are demanding more credits be given to them
And are unreasonable; we will not negotiate further

We call the realtor and tell him this is final
If they want out we will find another buyer
They finally realize what a deal they are getting
We have reached the deadline hour

We ride home quietly and I am quite tired
I rest for the balance of the day
It is soon time to eat our dinner
And I am grateful for having a good day

I head off to bed to finish a book
That I started earlier in the week
It is good to lose myself in a good read
It takes my mind off pain so bleak

June 19th

We awake to a bright and sunny day
And I feel much brighter too
Together we spend time in the yard
Weeding and planting as we do

Wilbur makes planters out of anything
And is happy to plant more flowers
I am content to weed the stone patio
And am proud of the work in a few hours

We work together quite well indeed
It is still a surprise to both of us
That we can really have fun while working
And know it is satisfying without any fuss

We are truly fortunate to have found each other
At this late stage in both of our lives
But we treasure each and every day together
We are aware of what we have now and are wise

We have been given another day to spend
Together and do as we please
We choose to spend in working side by side
Outside in the sunshine and cool breeze

June 20th

It is another bright and sunny morning
But rather cooler outside
Wilbur again works out in the yard
While I choose to rest inside

I am a little tired from yesterday
And realize that although I had fun
I should not overdue today
Despite the urge to have fun

I walk around the yard and admire
The work we have done thus far
The memorial rose garden is in full bloom
And the most spectacular by far

The flowers are colorful and growing well
Along with the vegetable garden
I can't wait to eat the peas and tomatoes
And the rest of the good things to come

A garden is indeed a magical sight
For from those tiny little seeds
We will be able to feed ourselves
If I can keep up with the weeds

It reminds me to take care of myself
And not allow too much stress in
To fuel my body and mind with only
The best of all possible things

I look forward to many better days ahead
When there will be less and less pain
And many more days of feeling well
With more strength for me to gain

I realize how delicate life really is
As I look forward once more
I hope my brother will fully recover
And be able to play an encore

June 21st

It is the beginning of another new week
And I am fortunate indeed
For I have been blessed these past few days
With peace, little pain, and time to read

We have finally reached the final phase
Of negotiating the sale of the house
The buyers now realize that we will not
Be treated like a country mouse

I must travel to Manchester later this week
To sign the final papers to please
We look forward to closing and having this done
So that we can move Bert in with ease

He is anxious to have this sale close
For the proceeds will fund the addition
Which we are planning so that he can live
Independently, improved healthy and fun

We are grateful to God just another time
That we are in a position to assist
My dear brother Bert with a place to live
And to give his spirit a huge lift

June 22nd

Today is our monthly anniversary
It is 7 years and 7 months today
I am busy with things around the house
Tonight is aerobics class to complete the day

I am working hard to adhere to my limits
Although it is very hard to do
My mind wants to follow a different path
But my body reminds me who is who

I speak with my brother on the phone
And learn that I must travel tomorrow
To sign the last of the house papers
Which are required by the buyer to borrow

We will meet with the realtor and both sign
And will be happy to be done at last
Now we just need to move dear Bert
Close on the house and leave the past

The church is planning a huge farewell
For Bert will be missed by everyone
I'm glad the entire Parish is invited
And that way they won't miss anyone

It's now the end of the day and time to rest
The class went exceptionally well
I can feel myself getting stronger at last
The Doctor will be pleased I'm happy to tell

Thank you dear God for another day
That was almost entirely without pain
I'm happy that when the pain does strike
I am able to withstand the strain

June 23rd

I sleep in until almost nine o'clock
And take my time in the shower
I eat a breakfast of good granola
And leave at the appropriate hour

The drive is pleasant although tiring
I've been doing this a few times each week
I try to avoid the rush hour traffic
Which proves to be an enormous feat

I take my brother to the pharmacy
To fill up one of his meds
He has made stuffed artichokes for lunch
What a treat for my stomach and head

We learn the news of our dear friend Don
Who was just diagnosed with Lung Cancer
We are all sorry to hear this sad news
It seems there is simply no answer

He will undergo treatment beginning at once
And will have a long struggle ahead of him
But he has the strength and the will to live
So perhaps the future is not so grim

We add him to the growing prayer list
It seems to be getting so long
That I've put the names in a "Prayer Jar"
And lift everyone up in a song

It's time now for me for the long drive home
And it is not too difficult this time
I have begun the trip earlier than usual
And find the ride to be sublime

I take the time to look at the scenery
The beauty of it lasts in my mind
The drivers seem not so crazy with speed
And I am surprised that they seem so kind

June 24th

Wilbur is traveling to New York City
And I have the day to do as I please
My daughter Alayne has driven out
And we plan a day of shopping with ease

She has brought me a plaque as a surprise
It's a teapot filled with tulips inside
The inscription is touching and moves me
She has opened up; I am filled with pride

We have not always seen eye to eye
But she is showing me that she is truly sincere
She is no longer afraid to express herself
And I find myself moved to tears

We go to the craft shop she has selected
We both make our purchases and then
We head off to the Christmas Tree shop
She has truly become a very good friend

We stop for some lunch to fuel ourselves
And then it's off to the bakery
She buys some bread and "dirtbombs"
And leaves one for Wilbur to eat

We have a great day and I realize
How blessed I am to have her
As a daughter and friend to have and hold
For the past, present and forever

June 25th

Today is the busiest day in months
I begin by cleaning out some drawers of jewelry
It takes me almost two hours time
To sort through the piles so thoroughly

I have accumulated way too many things
And must choose what to keep or throw away
It is not difficult to part with some of the pieces
While others bring old memories and must stay

Then we head to the computer store
For Wilbur's new computer will not print
We stop at the health food store for meds
And then pick up the trailer for the week

We will travel to Manchester again on Sunday
To bring over some things for the tag sale
And pick up my parents' old bedroom set
Which I want to keep; it has such fine detail

Then I begin two loads of laundry
And fold them and put them away
Then it's back to the computer store again
To pick up the restored computer on the way

Then we head back to the pharmacy
To pick up my two refills
It seems like this day will never end
And I come upstairs to write at my will

We have a late supper and watch some TV
And I phone my brother at long last
He tells me that he has been sick all day
And I wish there were a spell I could cast

He and I are both in pain now
For I carry his burden with me
But his will be with him for quite a long time
While mine is merely temporary

June 26th

Yesterday's work has taken its toll
I sleep in quite late this morning
I forgot that emptying all the drawers
And putting the clothes in boxes for storing

Has caused me a little muscle fatigue
And the weather is rainy and dark
The barometer must be awfully low
I am feeling the pain in every spot

I have a good breakfast to start the day
And plan to rest up and read
I realize that yesterday I over-worked
Now I must respond to my body's need

I've completed three books in two weeks time
And now have begun on the fourth
Reading is so therapeutic for me
I easily find myself completely lost

The stories take my mind off myself
And remind me of the good in the world
This is a truly great thing for me
It's another story to be told

I will rest up today for tomorrow's trip
Will be long and tiring both ways I'm afraid
But I'm looking forward to seeing my brother
And hopefully he'll be feeling better than yesterday

I continue to be both thrilled and amazed
At the good things that surround us all
The simple good wishes of many friends
And the time they take to call

June 27th

It is Sunday morning and we get ready to leave
We are traveling to my brother's today
We'll be moving some things out to the garage
To get ready for the tag sale on Saturday

I polish and clean the years of dust
Which have left things so dirty and marred
I wonder if anything will remove the grime
But I continue to remove the scars

Bert is outside with Wilbur this day
Picking out which plants will be moved
They finally come inside and see
The progress I've made, they are amused

Amy and Olivia are visiting also
And that is good for Bert's spirit
To have his niece and grandniece spend time with him
Tires him out but he is glad for the visit

We load up my parent's old bedroom set
And bring it home for our guestroom
I am reminded of my dear mother and father
And am unprepared for my reaction of gloom

I find myself crying as I carry up the drawers
And can actually see my mother
Sitting so clearly at the vanity desk
Putting cream on her face for cover

She had beautiful skin and I am blessed
To have inherited this skin from her
She never once in her life looked her age
And I've been blessed to look quite like her

I'm emotionally drained at the end of the day
And quite physically tired as well
I find myself crying deep into the night
Before I succumb to be quiet and still

June 28th

Another trip to Manchester again
Starts the beginning of another day
We drop off Wilbur's car to be fixed
And arrive at my brother's today

His car is also scheduled for a tune-up
And so we drive to the dealership to drop
Bert's car off for the work to be done
And then come back to finish the work

Now we are tagging each item for sale
And have some good laughs along the way
I bring up the bicycle from the shed
And fall up the hill so gracefully I'd say

My brother is worried that I've hurt myself
I assure him that I'm quite okay
I've bruised both my shins and they start to swell
We both laugh at how clumsy I am today

Wilbur teases me and says I should name
All the bruises I have on my legs
Like "Grace", "Balance" and "Agility"
It's a wonder they're not wooden pegs

We finally pick up Bert's car and return
And leave for the long drive home
We stop to pick up Wilbur's car on the way
And when I get home I phone

I let Bert know that we've arrived in one piece
And he asks me again if I'm hurt
I manage to convince him just once again
That I'm truly just a clumsy jerk

June 29th

I stayed up very late into the night
Watching reruns of Law & Order
By the time I managed to crawl into bed
It was past midnight a quarter

I fell asleep quite easily
The first time in such a long time
That when I awake this morning
I find it is well past nine

My body is stiff and really sore
I guess the fall took its toll
For I am very tired indeed
And black and blue where I rolled

I decide to stay at home and rest
For Wilbur has an appointment to see
A new doctor today for ear and nose
Who will find a cure, hopefully

His snoring has gotten so severe
That I'm afraid he's not getting enough air
Besides the fact that his snoring is so loud
Is beginning to be more than I can bear

It's a good day to rest; it's sunny and cool
And I find my way into a new book
And later this evening I plan to attend
Aerobics class if I can possibly look

And feel a little better than I do now
I want to continue to build up my strength
For only if I push myself a bit
Will I feel the results at long, long length

June 30th

We are halfway through the year today
I can hardly believe this much time
Has passed before my very eyes
I am happy and feel I'm doing fine

It's been such a long while that I've been home
Since last October, it feels like forever
I never realized that healing my body
Would take so much time; not ever

The problem is that I'm still not recovered
And I guess that is in God's plan
For I have always taken my health
A day at a time with no plan

There have been too many interruptions
With surgeries and broken bones
That I thought my time in healing was done
And I could simply move right along

I'm wiser now and find I must wait
For healing does not come overnight
No matter what plan I see for myself
God's plan is always right

And so mid-year I have learned quite a bit
About dealing with so much pain
That I no longer move in fast-forward
I have slowed down my body and brain

July 1st

Today is bright and sunny outside
What a perfect way to begin July
I'm feeling so good I can hardly believe
My spirit seems at an all time high

I received two notes in the mail yesterday
Both letting me know I am loved indeed
One was a thank you for a poem
The other a note card with a bag of tea

With a message to take time for myself
To relax in my sometimes hectic days
It was from my dear daughter Alayne
I am thrilled in so many different ways

I'll be seeing the Doctor later this morning
For a checkup on my progress so far
I think that she will be very pleased
I keep challenging myself and raising the bar

Later today I will mail the first half
Of the book draft of which this is a part
To my good and dear friend John Sherer
To enlist his help and support

I need to find a reliable agent
Who will read and edit my words
So that it possibly will be sent off
To a publisher who is interested in my work

I'm still in some pain from the fall I took
Last week while at my brother's
Although a fall usually brings about
A fight with my Fibromyalgia

I have managed again to sustain a fall
And the damage without too much pain
Although I can tell by the weather report
We soon will be getting some rain

July 2nd

Wilbur has picked up the Brass Headboard
So that I can begin to put together
The guestroom that will be temporary home
For now to my dearest brother

We hope to start the addition soon
And I am already anxious to begin
For when it is finally completed at last
Bert will have a new place to move in

We will all have to make some new adjustments
And I have taken on the new role
Of patient advocate for my brother
To secure the very best care for him in our locale

The time is drawing nearer each day
For the closing to be finally done
And when it is closed at long, long last
We will know we have finally won

We hope his battle with cancer goes well
And that he continues to respond
To treatments required whatever they be
And that he keeps his will to live on

I myself continue to improve
And I think attitude plays an important part
Of recovery and healing from any disease
One must believe with all one's heart

I am truly blessed to have this time
It has proven so special and dear
That I have been given this chance to write
About all my hopes and fears

I certainly hope it will serve to help
Many others who find themselves lost in pain
To motivate and inspire them to push forward
And continue on the path of good health again

July 3rd

I look forward to the rest of the year
When my writing will be completed and done
Putting down words of comfort on paper
I feel as if my best work is yet to come

I began this project in hopes of healing
The diseases with which I live
But they will be with me for the rest of my life
And so I am driven instead to give

The gift of myself to others in need
In the form of writing these words
They have been so rewarding to me so far
And I hope others will feel free as the birds

To try new things and have new hopes
That darkness and pain are not always present
For dreams with which to follow along
That relief is always in sight if you seek it

The world is really a wonderful place
Where we have been graced to reside
We need not look outside of ourselves
The truth always lies inside

July 4th

To my dear Granddaughter
KENDRA

Today marks the day of the birth of our Nation
It happens to be your birthday too
You are now entering your teen years today
And I am so very proud of you

You have become quite a young lady
With much love to give and receive
You are also an excellent basketball player
In whom many others have come to believe

Your gentleness and kindness always shine through
Wherever you go and whatever you do
The entire world is a much better place
Because of the likeness of you

You are smart and talented in many ways
You have been that way since you were born
Always looking to help everyone else
While never seeking any reward

My wish for you is for you to succeed
In each endeavor you undertake
And that you continue to love and be blessed
In whatever path you choose to take

I love you so much; you make me forget
The pain that I live with each day
Everyone should have someone like you
You're a bright shining light along the way

July 5th

Today we relax and enjoy the memory
Of the wonderful party we attended yesterday
To celebrate life for everyone present
And remember our Country's birthday

Karen and Mark & Reine and Steve
Were the hosts for the celebration
We ate and danced to our hearts' content
And paid tribute to the birth of our Nation

A fun day indeed was had by all
It was truly a remarkable day
To listen to music by Nick and Nancy
Made it spectacular needless to say

This morning we headed out the door
To pick up the final things we need
For Bert's room to be comfortable for him
We know that he will be pleased

We enjoy the day and I take time to rest
When we finally arrive back home
For dancing at the party yesterday
Left me quite tired right down to the bone

We are getting excited for very soon
Bert will be residing here with us
And we will ensure that he gets the best care
Quite easily and without too much fuss

We pray for Bert and for the others we know
The many who are dealing with cancer
But we will continue to storm the heavens
Until we receive some good answers

We hope they come soon and with some relief
For the pain and anguish we are feeling
Are hard to bear and it seems we are helpless
We continue to pray for hope and healing

July 6th

Today I will pick out some candles to match
The snuffer we bought for Alayne & Brian
They will celebrate their 13th anniversary soon
We are so happy for them we are smiling

Our children have made us very proud
They are raising their boys with such love
May God continue to bless them all
With peace and kindness from above

I will visit tomorrow with Alayne and the boys
Before they leave for their trips
Ethan will be traveling with "People To People"
Graham will be camping with his other grandparents

They both will be gone for two weeks time
Ethan will fly off to California
As a representative from Connecticut
There will be 46 children all together

Graham will have some special time alone
With Brian's parents who are wonderful
They will do many things that will be fun
And I'm sure also very educational

How fortunate they are this special family
They are all loved so very much
My daughter has chosen after quite some time
To remain closer and more in touch

I am truly blessed and don't ever forget
Nor do I take my life for granted
For I understand now the true meaning of
The phrase to "Bloom where you are planted"

July 7th

Today begins a bit early for me
I will drive to Alayne's this morning
Then we will go to Manchester again
To pack up the rest of Bert's belongings

We begin packing the lava lamps
And are really stunned to discover
That 200 feet of bubble wrap
Is barely just enough to cover

The lamps, which fill up six boxes in all
Together with their bases and frames
We share a good laugh to see so many
The boys want to know if they're games

We explain that their value is quite a lot
In common dollars and cents
Now they are much more interested
And want to search the Internet

Next we pack up the kitchen supplies
And find a lot of things to throw out
The packing and lifting of so many boxes
Has left us quite tired and worn-out

And so we begin the trip back home
And stop at the health food store
So I can pick up the things I need
To help my body and mind to restore

I nap for a while when I reach home at last
It has been such a busy day
But I am grateful to be able to help
With my daughter and grandsons along the way

Tonight I will rest and not do too much
I must save my strength for Friday
Wilbur and I will bring Bert here
For his summer interim stay

July 8th

Today begins with laundry to do
For I want to be able to be free
For the rest of the day and aerobics class
And the busy weekend ahead you see

The small move is slated for Friday afternoon
While the official move is scheduled for Sunday
Most things will be put in storage for now
Until the addition is well on its way

I have pushed too far and I am aware
That my body is paying the price
But it seems to me such a small price to pay
To ensure the happiness of my brother's life

I am trying to pace myself along the way
With wisdom and knowing my limits
But it is too easy to forget them for now
And push all the harder to get this finished

We will all be happy when this move is done
And Bert has a new home to live in
Now I pray for his strength and recovery
For the cancer that lives within him

He will have great new Doctors in town
Who will treat him with the very best care
I know for a fact that our new cancer center
Is rated higher than others with which to compare

July 9th

Today is Friday the day to pick up Bert
And bring him home to our farm
We pack up some remaining things he has
Some come in the house; others to the barn

The ride goes fairly smoothly I'd say
Despite the busy traffic in the city
But once we arrive out to the country
Things move along rather quickly

We all pitch in to unload the things
And designate where they will go
We have a late dinner of pasta and sauce
Then it's off to bed we all go

We are all tired out and ready for sleep
From the long events of the day
We hug Bert good night and welcome him home
For now he is here to stay

I say my prayers in silence tonight
There are so many things to pray for
Peace, respite and return to health
Not to mention the other requests before

I fall asleep in the middle of talking
To Wilbur the love of my life
I can't remember what we were talking about
But I think it was about relief being in sight

July 10th

We all sleep in a little late today
Which is truly a great blessing
For tomorrow we go back to Manchester
To help load the trucks for moving

We head off to Amy's to help celebrate
Kendra's 13th birthday this afternoon
She has all her basketball girlfriends there
And there are presents all around us soon

Kendra does not seem happy today
I wonder what the problem is really?
Carlos comes early to pick up Olivia
As she is clinging on tight to her Mommy

We have sandwiches, salads and chips to eat
And then Kendra opens her presents
I wish she were smiling but she seems sullen
We meet all of her girlfriends' parents

We leave after the party is over and done
And return home to see how my brother is
For he was too weak to make the trip
And stayed home to be with the kitty

The day ends quietly as we go to bed
Everyone is tired and spent
We thank God for all the blessings
Which upon us He has sent

July 11th

Today is moving day here at last
Bert stays at home to rest
There is really nothing for him to do
We all work at our very best

We wrap the furniture in plastic wrap
To protect it while it is in storage
This process takes up most of the day
When we arrive home we are exhausted

Fred has loaded the moving van
And we fill up Arlene's truck as well
Wilbur's truck can hold no more
We are glad to be done; this is hell

We order pizza for everyone to share
The effort has been long and hard
Tomorrow we must go back and clean
And bring back some plants for the garden

We finally finish up for the day
And are glad this day is over
We all clean up with showers and baths
And look forward to tomorrow

July 12th

Today we head back just once again
To the empty house to clean
The men head outside to dig the plants
I sweep and polish the kitchen to gleam

This takes more time than we had allotted
And we must also stop at the pharmacy
We take some time for a very late lunch
And then head for home happily

I find myself in great pain again
And know that I've pushed too far
I'm glad to discover that it's only Monday
For I can relax once I'm out of the car

These frequent trips have taken their toll
I'm tired, crabby and not really myself
But tomorrow will come and with it relief
I can finally take some time for soul and self

And so we arrive home fatigued and tired
But with a great sense of accomplishment
We do not have to visit the house again
That fact brings us all enjoyment

July 13th

Today is a day of rest for us all
I take advantage and sleep in late
Bert unpacks a few more boxes
And I simply relax and wait

It is Alayne and Brian's anniversary
I have already sent a gift
But I take the time to call them up
My spirit needs a little lift

I tell them today they are doubly blessed
Because it's their thirteenth year
The thirteenth year and the thirteenth day
I love them both; they are so very dear

It's aerobics night and I feel much better
And happy that I have the strength
To go and bounce around the floor
It is absorbing and I am no longer tense

I work quite hard in class tonight
I guess I'm working off feeling grouchy
I lift my weights and work my muscles
When I come home my joints are ouchy

I take a shower to cool myself down
And relax as the water falls on me
It is like the blessing of the quiet rain
Only it is falling down softly upon me

Things are almost over with the house
And for this I am very thankful indeed
Tomorrow we will drive to the closing at last
And hand over the keys and the deed

July 14th

The day for the closing is finally here
But I am distressed to discover
That out favorite attorney has fallen ill
And taken to the hospital to recover

Instead Arlene will handle the closing
She is capable and could do this in her sleep
I'm glad she is coming but concerned as well
For Allan Thomas' health, he is so very sweet

He is not charging us any fee at all
For I worked with him for five years
I'm glad that we have chosen a nice gift
And send it off with some tears

The closing goes well I'm happy to say
But we must go back to Manchester again
For we asked to have certified funds
And Allan's office will have to provide them

We make this last drive quite easily
And find Allan's wife in his office making calls
We give her the gift; she will take it to Allan
She says it will make his night and lift his pall

We bid our farewells to everyone
With check in hand we take off for home
It is too late to deposit the check today
For when we arrive the Bank is closed

We count our blessings once again
To have this deal finally close
We wished the new owners the best of luck
And now we can move forward with New Hope

July 15th

The day begins busy just once again
As I'm ready to head off to the Bank
The cable man arrives to install a new cable
I forgot he was coming and my heart sank

I left Bert in charge for the little I know
Of the cable and how it works
The cable-man asked to drill in the floor
I said do whatever will work

Then I drove myself to the Bank
To deposit our funds from the sale
I returned to find the cable-man still here
He and Bert were chatting happily away

Then it was time to call my dear Amy
And wish her a happy birthday
I dropped off her gifts at Kendra's party
Which took place last Saturday

She was happy to here from Bert and me
I asked her if she felt any older, she's my baby
To have my youngest child turn thirty eight
Makes me feel like a little old lady

She laughed and told me she was only 29
And that I must have miscalculated
We shared a good laugh between ourselves
We both ended up feeling elated

It's aerobics night and I am still tired
But I will go to make myself feel better
For when I work out my muscles and joints
I know I am helping myself to heal quicker

So thank you God for the busy week
And all the blessings You have sent our way
We will go out to dinner tomorrow night
To celebrate our good fortune and be able to pay

July 16th

It is Friday morning and we all rest in
For the week has been busy enough
Tonight we will all go out to dinner
At a place called A. Joseph's'

I'm excited to know that I can finally take
My husband and brother to dinner
And not worry about the bill at all
We all will come out as winners

Bert and Wilbur play out in the garden
Planning some new flower beds
I decide to take a ride on the swing
When the rope breaks, I land like lead

Thank God I did not break my hip
Although the bruise is the size of South Asia
They both come to see if I'm really all right
I think I must be living in Fantasia

For this is the third time within a few weeks
That I have fallen and gotten hurt
But we go out to dinner anyway
I will not stop the fun planned for Uncle Bert

We listen to Nick and Nancy play
And get up to dance a few numbers
Our dinners are delicious to say the least
And we pack up all the leftovers

Nancy admires the cross I am wearing
So before we get up to leave
I remove it from my neck and ask that Wilbur
Place it around Nancy's neck; she is so pleased

We are all really tired from the events of the week
So we head out the door a little early
We bid our farewells and say goodbye
To all of our friends so dearly

July 17th

I am stiff and sore when I awake
The bruise has gotten even bigger
I put some topical cream on it
Hoping to make it feel better

It is Jeanette's 91st birthday and so we go
To pick her up and head for Mary Jane's
For she has planned a party for her mother
And we participate among family and friends

Wilbur's mother cannot believe her age
She didn't expect to live this long
But she is so very witty and wise
She is right where she belongs

Among her family, cousins and friends
We celebrate her 91 years
With a lovely party, gifts and cards
Along with a few shed tears

We thank everyone and head for home
It is a one and one-half hour drive
We are both exhausted and tired
When at home we finally arrive

Bert asks how the party went
We tell him it was just fine
Tomorrow we will go to St. James Church
To honor Bert's work with parishioners in line

We head up the stairs and go to bed
For we are all tired and spent
We look forward to tomorrow with hope
And know that it will be a great event

July 18th

Today is the day we go to celebrate
All of Bert's fine accomplishments
There are sandwiches, salads and a giant cake
And platters full of refreshments

The people file in a few at a time
And soon the hall is filled to the brim
Monsignor gets up to make a short speech
And Bert gets a standing ovation

Bert gets up and says, "thanks, it was fun"
But I know he is too moved to speak
So I pick up the microphone to say a few words
And when I'm finished I find myself weak

This has been Bert's life for so long
He is embarrassed by all the attention
But he deserves every bit of it and more
Without him the parish will not function

I've never been so proud of my brother before
He is loved by everyone in attendance
We stay for the entire afternoon
And head home with gifts in abundance

We arrive home late in the day
And I play secretary while he opens his gifts
He cannot believe what he has received
And I know his spirit has been given a lift

The parishioners have proved to be generous
He has over $4,000 in gift money
Along with the presents and Mass Cards
He is blessed and will be sadly missed by many

We rest for a while and have dinner late
We are all still quite moved with emotion
The people have shown their love for Bert
I feel so happy, proud and pleased for him

July 19th

I sleep in late I am still very sore
But I am relishing yesterday's party
For finally Bert received the proper recognition
For all his hard work in the Parish

Not only was he the music director
But chef and bookkeeper as well
His music is what will be missed the most
However; the priests are skinny as hell

They have tried a number of cooks already
And nobody can match Bert's skill
He loves to cook and now is enjoying
Someone cooking for him as well

He has been puttering around outside the yard
With Wilbur close at his side for assistance
They are planning just where to plant the things
He has dug up from the house in Manchester

I stay indoors and change the sheets
On both Bert's bed and ours
I'm doing loads of laundry today
I feel a good sense of today's hours

I'm still feeling stiff and quite sore yet
I know that this pain will pass
I wish it would hurry along its way
I want to feel better too fast

I received a call from the office today
It was a sad call indeed
Jean said that since the time I've been gone
There has been no display of humanity

I know that God's will was to remove me
From the toxic environment there
And focus on writing and spending more time
On myself and my brother in prayer

July 20th

Today I awake reeling in pain
The bruise on my hip is a left over token
I had my shoulder x-rayed yesterday
To be certain that it was not broken

When the swing broke and I fell to the ground
I knew right away that I was hurt
But I went right along with our plans anyway
And now I feel like such a jerk

I think the bruise is really dangerous
It is over three inches in diameter
It is swollen and very sore to the touch
It will be a long time until it is better

My shoulder hurts also and it has a bruise
I thought I had chipped a bone
But the doctor phoned me early this morning
To say that it was not broken at all

I do all Bert's laundry, three loads in all
And pack up some boxes for moving
There is still some space in the storage unit
For the things he will not be using

I'm tired and disappointed in myself
Falling seems to have become too natural
I know that the falls have been accidents
But I'm tired and want to be normal

And so I must rest for the next few days
And cannot attend aerobics class
This always annoys the heck out of me
I want my recovery to be speedy and fast

And so I'm resigned to rest and to pray
There are people much worse off than me
I'll simply refocus on resting myself
And continue writing this poetry

July 21st

I'm hoping today will be much improved
From the way I felt yesterday
I need to feel more positive
In my outlook and feeling this way

I so dislike spending days in pain
It is as though the days are wasted
I want to feel stronger and stronger each day
And not be forced to become quiet and tested

Perhaps I'm not listening to God very well
And the only way to get my attention
Is to force me to slow down and listen
To His words of long sought wisdom

More than half the year has passed me by
And yet I still seem to come up short
You'd think after this much time had passed
I would have learned how to be a good sport

I guess I still don't want to feel so sick
It's as though I'm not totally complete
I know for certain that any illness
Is not a sign of being weak

The message is clear in my head
It has not yet moved to my heart
God must be so very patient with me
I have been so stubborn from the start

I make these promises to myself
And then fail to adhere to what I know
I ask for more patience for myself
The learning process is so very slow

Thank you God for the lessons you give
I promise to make a better effort
I know that I must continue to slow down
And that You are there for support

July 22nd

Today I will visit Doc Spiegel again
I can just imagine his reaction
To the bruises and falls of the last few weeks
He will tell me to cool the action

Thank goodness Wilbur will accompany me
For he is always there for support
I don't know how I would manage these trips
Without him to help me to talk

I always seem to forget important things
That the Doctor really needs to know
But when I'm in pain I can't remember
My brain seems to find another place to go

Perhaps this is the way my body reacts
To somehow dismiss the pain
For if I acknowledge the reality of it
I'm sure it would be too taxing on my brain

I simply cannot accept this as God's will
It is as though I am being punished
I know that God would not do this to me
I'm somehow simply being blessed

We will stop by the bank for a short visit
I have a small gift for my friend Ed
Who has accepted a teaching position
Way to go friend and move ahead

He's been studying now for three long years
To obtain his certificate to teach
He'll be teaching French at the high-school level
Lucky are the kids to whom he will reach

I was blessed to have him in my employ
For he is energetic, faithful and smart
I wish the absolute very best for him
A brand new life for him to start

July 23rd

Well, what a surprise I had yesterday
When the Doc said just as I had predicted
To lay off my feet and rest for a while
It's as though I had his speech scripted

He said that the bruise on my thigh
Was a very deep muscle injury
The kind that they take football players
Off the field and treat immediately

The fact that I'm only half the size
Of a very small football player
Makes the injury twice as bad
There isn't enough tissue and layers

He thinks that although my shoulder isn't broken
There could very well be that it's chipped
I can either live with the chip and scar tissue
Or see an Orthopaedic surgeon to go in and find it

I think I'll choose to just live with it
I am not in any hurry to have surgery
Which would set me back even further
On my plan to full recovery

He suggested I double the Vioxx I'm taking
And do nothing for the next few weeks
How simply he utters these words of doom
While my blood pressure is reaching its peak

But in the end I know he is right
And today I feel a little bit better
Tonight we will take the kids out to dinner
And thank them for being such good helpers

July 24th

It's the beginning of the weekend
And I sleep in very late
Dinner with the kids last night was fun
And a huge amount of food I ate

Ethan was all aglow from his trip
From the beautiful state of California
He had tales to tell about the many places
They visited and how he enjoyed them

Graham had his own special tales to tell
From his trip to Acadia National Park
He spent nearly two weeks time
Camping with Grandma and Grandpa

All in all it was a wonderful time
Spent with our daughter's family
Brian had his tales of hiking and camping
And due to the weather coming home early

Alayne managed to paint their bedroom
And then when she was finished
Decided to tackle the living room as well
She has energy unbounded and unlimited

Thank you dear Lord for our family
And the time we spend together
It was a good dinner but best of all
Was the chance to get out for my brother

July 25th

The day does not begin very well
I got very little sleep last night
I came up to the loft for peace and quiet
And stayed up almost half the night

I crawled back into bed at 4:30 AM
And slept only until about ten
The pain monster is rearing its ugly head
Due to not enough good sleep again

Arlene and Fred are driving out today
To bring Bert his remaining things
He and Wilbur have been planting fools
Making new beds for flowers and digging

Wilbur will grill pork chops outside
I can't wait until they arrive
They are so busy with everything else
And I know it's a very long drive

Later today Wilbur will leave for New York
To work there for the next few days
He'll return on Wednesday afternoon
I hope he will receive lots of praise

His work has become quite busy of late
And he is both nervous and happy
To juggle his time between work and play
Is difficult to do without a nappy

My week ahead looks busy indeed
With Dr. appointments for me and my brother
Thank God we have been able to set up
The time for the visits and each other

July 26th

Today marks the day of our father's birthday
He would have been one hundred two
Oh how I wish he were with us now
And seeing us all together too

He would be very proud of brother Bert
And all of his accomplishments
For Bert was always the talented one
Never seeking any acknowledgements

He would be happy to know and also see
That we are caring for one another
We have truly become the very best friends
Myself and Wilbur and my brother

I slept until noon being sleep deprived
And then slept the afternoon away
I feel like the sleep bug has bitten me hard
This has been one totally useless day

But sleep I needed and it is sleep I got
My body feels extremely weak
For when I finally awake again
I can barely stand up on my feet

Bert and I make a great dinner
And then we watch some TV
Before long I am off to bed
To catch up on some more zzzzzz's

I hope tomorrow that I'll feel refreshed
After spending most of the day a sleepy-head
Bert wants me to call the Doctor again
But I refuse, take a shower and go to bed

July 27th

Today I awake more peacefully
I slept all through the night
I come downstairs and have some coffee
And a small breakfast to set me a-flight

I go to pick up the garbage cans
And see that there is a disaster
There is garbage strewn all over the lawn
I get the rake and put it in the trashcan

I don't know if the raccoons have gotten it
Or if the garbage men were sloppy
But either way the mess is disgusting
So I clean it up and am not very happy

And so starts the day, oh boy I can't wait
To see what is next in line for us
As we need to run quite a few errands today
I hope we can do so without a lot of fuss

I'm still undecided about aerobics tonight
I'll just have to see how I am feeling
I do hope that I will be able to attend
Without my head rocking and reeling

Thank you God for the rest I have gotten
Although it was not what I planned
But You always know what is best for me
And so I leave myself in Your capable hands

July 28th

This day begins entirely different
I have recovered some energy
I did not attend class last night
I was still overly tired and not me

I had my appointment with Diane today
Who has been such a great help to me
And when I returned home I was surprised
To find out that Bert had driven to the pharmacy

He has not been able to drive his car
Since sometime early last March
I think this is tremendous progress
He is as happy as a lark

Tomorrow we will visit his new specialist
And bring all his records and notes along
The treatment thus far seems to have eased his pain
And I feel like singing a song

He is the one who has the cancer
While I continue to have much pain
This seems to be quite ridiculous to me
Just one more reminder that I'm not in control again

Wilbur returns home this afternoon
From his three days in New York City
He says the program was a huge success
I'm happy to simply sit and listen

I tell him of the events of the week
Which have transpired since he was gone
He listens to all the happy news
But bristles when I begin to complain

July 29th

Today begins quite cheerfully
I strip the beds and do laundry
Bert is a little nervous today
It is off to a new Doctor to see

I want to go inside with him and listen
To what the Doctor has to say
But I don't want to encroach on Bert's time
So I'll stay wherever he wants me to stay

We have some additional errands to run
And he wants to drive one way
I agree for him to take the wheel
And I'll drive home the other way

Bert's spirit seems upbeat and of that I'm glad
He could very easily look and feel like doom
But he is planning for his new place
I hope they get started really soon

I'm trying very hard to manage everything
But sometimes I feel like a failure
I have difficulty keeping my own spirit up
Perhaps this will come by trial and error

I'm grateful to not be in such pain
That I'm really able to serve
I need to keep a very close watch
On my intake and on my reserves

Thank you for this day of peace
And to have been given enough energy
Perhaps tonight I'll try to attend class
And participate, as I'm able to be

July 30th

I know I believe in miracles now
For today I've actually seen one
The specialist I took my brother to see
Turned out to be quite wonderful

He is the cousin of Bert's good friends
The DeVanney's who live in Manchester
They are the ones who donated the food
For the church party and celebration

Jim DeVanney is Tim's cousin
And brother to Bert's friend Ray
I came in with Bert to speak with him
And felt blessed when I walked away

He did not object to my being there
In fact he was greatly in favor of it
He said that four ears are better than two
And I could tell that Bert's spirit was lifted

I cannot express on paper with words
The feeling that this was God showing His face
I've seen things I thought were coincidence
But this was clearly an act of God's grace

July 31st

Today I'm meeting my daughter Alayne
We are dressing up to go and have tea
I feel like a little girl again
Playing dress-up and having a party

This was Alayne's idea and I'm pleased
We are spending more time together
I hope the day turns out just fine
And that we enjoy good weather

The teahouse she has chosen is in Wethersfield
An old town with much history
I am filled with anticipation and wonder
I've never before been to a formal tea

I know she will be surprised and happy
When I tell her about yesterday
She and Brian were at the church party
When Bert was honored in a very special way

To know that the world is a very small place
Is still a big surprise to me
Wilbur contends that if we went to the moon
I would find someone who would recognize me

I'm bringing Alayne a small token
I love being able to give gifts
She and I have been exchanging a few
During our last couple of visits

I'm bringing her a small silver cross
With a diamond as the center stone
Amy, Kendra and I each have one
And I want Alayne to have one of her own

August 1st

Today is Sunday and I'm still remembering
The fun we had yesterday
Our tea was actually a four-course lunch
Which we devoured quite easily

We had a great time; mother and daughter
Dressing up in our flowery dresses
The ladies all commented on how nice we looked
And my teapot purse caused many questions

However; I woke up very late indeed
It was almost noontime I'd say
And then I went back to bed at one
And slept the afternoon away

My shoulder was in a great deal of pain
And the massage and sleep seemed to work
For after I got up to eat my dinner
I was back in my bed by eight

Wilbur and Bert went out for a ride
And spent almost the entire day
Visiting the many sights to see
In the northwest corner of our state

I enjoyed the peace and quiet too
And turned off the phone by the bed
I intended to read some more of my book
But I fell back to sleep instead

Thank you God for the chance to rest
Although I would much rather be up
But You always know what is best for me
And so to You I lift myself up

August 2nd

Today the sun is shining brightly
I get up early and have breakfast
Soon Bert comes down the stairs
And he is hungry again at last

He seems to be improving more each day
And we are all happy about that
Because he looked so bad for a while
I'm glad to have my brother back

I wish they would hurry and get the approvals
Which are needed to begin the addition
But we keep running into little snags
That are frustrating—they all seem so little

But we must keep up hope that soon they'll begin
The process of digging and building
Wilbur has moved all the shrubbery around
So to clear the space for the addition

Today Bert and I will take a ride
To the health food store and then
We'll go looking for a computer store
Where he can purchase some items again

I hope this day ends as it has begun
With the sun shining down upon us
We all seem to have more energy
Today is another day to count blessings

August 3rd

It is Tuesday and the day for a haircut trim
I will go to see Doug this morning
This time my hair is really overgrown
To Doug it will seem more like mowing

He tells me that he's never before in his life
Seen anyone's hair grow like mine
I tell him it must be the vitamins I take
Too bad it doesn't work on my spine

The day goes along smoothly with nothing amiss
We are all tired of being warm and muggy
We want to go outside and work in the yard
But are unable to because it is too buggy

I go to aerobics class tonight eagerly
To see if I can truly keep up
I am pleased that we are doing intervals
Because that will mean no pushups

I do better than I thought and keep up the pace
My shoulder has loosened up quite a bit
I seem to be able to move more freely
But the weights are still difficult to lift

Thank you dear God for the chance to go out
And limber up my stiff body and soul
Although I enjoy the moving around
It is still quite an effort all in all

August 4th

Today is more pleasant although still warm
We all go outside to work in the yard
Wilbur and Bert are planting and spraying
While I choose weeding as my job

Most folks think I'm crazy to actually enjoy
The task of weeding the flowerbeds
But the results are amazing and I get to see
The rewards of my efforts just ahead

I find it relaxing to pull up the weeds
And see the clear mulch underneath
The roses look so bright and fresh
It's as though the bushes can really speak

They are saying thank you for freeing us from
The clutches of the strangling weeds
I think I can actually relate to the roses
And am releasing some memories with these deeds

Tonight Bert and I will go out for dinner
He has chosen a Mexican place to dine
I eat way too much and can hardly believe
The food was actually quite divine

I am happy for Wednesday's to come each week
Bert and I have some time to spend alone
Wilbur, Roger and Jack go out each Wednesday
And before Bert came I usually stayed at home

So now we can go out and enjoy our time
Together we are free to talk about things
This is truly a gift from God above
We both enjoy the healing it brings

August 5th

Today is the day Bert sees the Doctor
To check on his bladder improvement
Unfortunately there seems to be none
In fact he now has a urine infection

The doctor prescribes a new antibiotic
And a drug that will stop the burning
But Bert does not have a good reaction
And so he spends the entire day hurting

This has me worried and I do not sleep well
Despite the aerobics class I attend
That usually burns me out to the point
Where I find myself totally spent

I come home and jump into the warm shower
To take away some of the pain
The water feels so healing to me
Like a quiet, soft summer rain

I take my meds and head off to bed
To quietly read for awhile
I turn on the CD player and listen
To soft relaxing music and I smile

How fortunate am I to have this time
To spend with my husband and brother
We have become a true family of three
Each of us supporting one another

August 6th

It is Friday again and Fosamax day
I awake and take my meds
Since I had trouble sleeping last night
I really want to stay in my bed

But I get up with courage to start the new day
There is always something good if I look
I peddle my bike for one half hour
The time passes while I begin a new book

The house was cleaned yesterday thanks to Deb
Who comes once every other week
Since I am not able to do the chores
Which are necessary to maintain the upkeep

I am feeling better and in not so much pain
I'm working very hard to be strong
The process is difficult and takes much time
I realize this and simply go along

I'm reminded again whose timetable I'm on
It clearly is not in my power
God is in charge of time and space
I must simply follow by the hour

No matter how long I still feel blessed
To have this time to recover
I'm learning new things every day
About love and its overwhelming power

August 7th

Today it is breezy, sunny and cool
A perfect day to work in the yard
So that is what I intend to do
Weeding is sometimes so hard

But today I am filled with energy
A surplus from I'm not sure where
And so I tackle the new lily beds
And fill in with cedar mulch everywhere

Next is the tangled overgrown mess
Of what was once the pretty rock-garden
I can't even tell the plants from the weeds
So I pull up everything and enlarge it

I keep trying to make the circle look good
And in my efforts I find out
That I continue to make the circle larger
Than it was when I first started out

This is OK because Bert wants to plant
New bulbs that will bloom in the spring
This will be quite a beautiful spot
For tulips and daffodils in a ring

Tonight we prepare for our trivia game
For we are the hosts this time
We are happily surprised and did not know
That Judy and Jack would arrive

Bert came down and had dinner with us all
This made me so happy indeed
Because he is not feeling well at all
And did so that I might be pleased

Thank you God for family and friends
Who warm our hearts and our home
We know if we place our trust in You
We are never truly alone

August 8th

I'm tired from staying up so late
But the game proved to be lots of fun
Bert won the game for the men this time
The women had trouble from question one

I get up and head down the stairs
For coffee and a small breakfast
Today our friend Carmen will visit with us
We are pleased to have her as our guest

Carmen is very special indeed
We met at the seminar last year
She is bright and willing to share with us
Which is a far cry from all the past tears

She used to be quiet and very private
With a lot of leftover hurt still inside
But the seminar and friends changed all that
And now we are all filled with pride

Wilbur has baked small fruit tarts
To serve us later this afternoon
He has taken over the baking job
And I find myself relaxed and cool

He is so very good and loving to me
And to my brother as well
We could not ask for better treatment
He shares his love very well

Thank you for this loving man in our lives
He seems to know just what to do
Whenever he senses that I don't feel well
He takes over whatever job there is to do

August 9th

Today I awake in excruciating pain
It is Fibromyalgia visiting again
My ribcage is completely on fire
I feel like I'm being stuck with pins

The nerve endings seem to short circuit
While firing off all at the same time
I take some pain meds and rest all day
I cannot believe this pain is mine

Wilbur comes up to rub lotion on my ribs
The friction relieves some of the pain
The nerve endings fire off their energy
And I finally find some relief once again

This attack has struck out of the blue
I am amazed at its intensity
I don't think that I overworked myself
And I don't like this pain one bit

I finally take a shower and head up to bed
I have accomplished nothing today
But rest and cry and feel disappointed
That I have somehow failed again someway

My brother and Wilbur come talk to me
And comfort me and calm me down
They tell me that nothing is required of me
Except to relax and lay down

I do as instructed and find relief
Thank God for my wonderful family
Who have the good sense to speak the truth
And finally get through to me

August 10th

Today is filled with much less pain
And I can get up and move around
I spend the day changing sheets on the beds
And doing the piles of laundry on the ground

Bert is feeling better and that is good
He takes himself out for a drive
He goes to the pharmacy and tools around
And brings me home a surprise

A set of healing candles to burn
I light one and ponder the smell divine
It helps to relieve the pain I feel
And also relaxes my mind

Wilbur makes a fabulous dinner
Baked chicken, potatoes and beans
Picked fresh today from the garden
They are ever so tender and green

Bert's "Angel Trumpet" plant is flowering
It is quite something to behold
I've never seen anything like it before
As the fragrance sweetly unfolds

All in all we are really quite blessed
We are able to support one another
What a gift it is to have Bert here
I am truly learning to appreciate my brother

August 11th

Bert is supposed to see Dr. DeVanney today
But something has gone amiss
The office calls to reschedule the time
And that is certainly OK with us

We have a few errands to run
So we go to town and complete them
We return home to find that the appointment we had
Needs to be cancelled and rescheduled

This is not good, as Bert's gout has appeared
And he's not feeling well at all
We leave another message with the office
To have Dr. DeVanney return our call

He calls in a prescription to the pharmacy
And so we go out once again
It's not as though it was a trip to the corner
It is ten miles to go and come back again

Bert takes his medicine but gets little relief
He goes upstairs to lie down for a while
When dinner is ready to eat, so is he
And he comes down the stairs with a smile

In the meantime, I have been bitten nine times
By a very nasty mosquito or fly
I have puncture wounds all over my arm
And the itching is making me cry

I try my formula of meat tenderizer
Mixed with an anti-itch cream
But the wounds are open to the air
The medicine burns and I scream

The burn is much better than the itch
So I repeat the procedure a few times
Hopefully this itch will slowly abate
And I'll feel better in time

August 12th

Bert and I are both feeling crummy
So we decide to do nothing but rest
Wilbur is out working someplace
My itching feels like a test

To see just how much pain I can endure
Before I scratch off my arm
I repeat the same procedure again
It lessens the burn for a while

Now I reach for the Benadryl
To stop the itching from inside
I feel like my body is filled with poison
I am tired of this itching besides

I am drowsy from the medicine
And choose not to attend class tonight
My energy level is truly at zero
And my mind is not far behind

So I watch some TV, eat and rest
And make some calls on the phone
This relaxes me for a little while
And then I return to the sleep zone

I suppose it is good to have some rest
But for me this pattern is getting tiresome
Why on earth can't I just feel well?
I'd like the answer to that one

August 13th

Today is Friday the 13th of August
Some have their superstitions
Our carbon monoxide alarm goes off
And we end up calling the firemen

They arrive very quickly and look around
They make sure everyone is out of the house
Then they go in and test the air
Everything is fine when they come out

The alarm has malfunctioned and it is time
To replace it and also get a second one
Which will be placed upstairs where we sleep
To ensure the safety of everyone

Bert has an appointment with Dr. Oltikar
And I drive him and sit with both of them
Filling in the blanks where necessary
Bert likes her and that is wonderful

She has been our favorite Doctor
For almost five years straight
She is kind and listens very well
And we never have long to wait

So all in all it's another exciting day
In the world of home and health
I wish some days were a little less exciting
And that we had a little more wealth

Wilbur is working a lot these days
And then he is traveling too
I don't like it when he goes to the city
It's a scary time these days this is true

So I pray my prayers in silence and tears
And hope for the best is all I can do
I know God is listening to what I ask
I hope He will answer me soon

August 14th

I sleep in late and when I awake
The itching is driving me crazy
I repeat my medicine just once again
And for the rest of the day I feel lazy

Wilbur comes home with his brand new truck
It is a bright shiny metallic color of red
I joke with him about speeding tickets
He laughs off my comments in his head

We have a nice dinner and I clean up
Load the dishwasher and head off to bed
Bert has a slightly elevated temperature
I am worried as I feel his head

I try not to think that things are getting worse
I so want him to enjoy his time here
I am getting impatient to begin the digging
But we must wait for the variance to appear

I lay awake well until past midnight
Praying and crying at the same time
I go downstairs to get something to drink
And I smell pipe smoke ever so fine

I go back to bed and tell Wilbur
His father must be here for a visit
It is then that I realize that this is the day
Five years ago he died, how we miss him

I ask his father what should I do?
He smiles and says I should sleep
There is nothing for me to do at all
It is in God's hands to keep

August 15th

Yes today is the 5th anniversary of Pop's passing
It is also the 4th year for Ollie the cat
This is too much sadness for my brain to handle
But I acknowledge this all and try not to snap

Later today Wilbur will leave for New York
To be working there until Wednesday to speak
I miss him when he leaves the day before
And I have trouble getting to sleep

The cats curl up beside me at night
It's as if they are there to protect me
I get up very early in the morning
And discover the prize they have left me

A little mouse is dead at my side
Lying very still on the floor
I am a little freaked out a bit
But I manage to carry him out the door

The cats are quite proud of themselves
They do this when Wilbur is away
They think they are taking good care of me
I wish they would find another way

Ella and Sarah are having quite a time
They don't know what to make of Mary
My brother's cat has taken over the house
And our cats find this a bit scary

But none-the-less we are all thankful
To have Bert stay here with us
Soon the building of his place will begin
And then will come all the fuss

August 16th

This morning begins too early for me
I go back to bed for more sleep
It comes quite easily for me this time
And I fall into a very deep sleep

When I finally get up I am very drowsy
And have some coffee to wake up
My feet are moving at a very slow pace
And I struggle to just keep up

There is nothing special on the calendar today
And I am truly grateful for that
My focus energy level is very low
And my energy is totally flat

I lay around and get into a book
And find myself dozing away
I wake up and think that this is a waste
Of a very beautiful day

But I am in pain and feel change coming
The weather here is not my friend
And so I take my meds again
And fall back to sleep again

God is protecting my sleepy head
From thinking too much about myself
Bert is not feeling too well at all
And I take it all upon myself

Wilbur calls and tells me to relax
That I am not responsible for everything
I know in my heart that this is true
But all I want is happiness to bring

I feel life again slipping through my hands
And know there is nothing I can do
Just simply accept what is to be
Learn to let go and let God shine through

August 17th

Today I call "Abbey Press" catalogue
To order the last few things
My Christmas shopping is almost complete
And the living room is filled to the brim

I am sorting the boxes by family
And trying to get things organized
But everything seems to be everywhere
And this task turns into quite a job

But now when new things arrive in the mail
I have a special place to put them
Pretty soon I will start the wrapping process
As soon as everything is in

I look around and think it is good
That I began shopping so early
There are so many things to wrap
I'll take it family by family

The biggest pile is for brother Bert
I want this Christmas to be special
I am feeling so very close to him
And I want him to feel love from us all

There is no aerobics class tonight
As Cindy is on vacation
I hope she is having a wonderful time
We all need a break and some recreation

August 18th

Wilbur is still in New York City
I'm missing him way too much
Although he calls me every night
I need to feel his soft touch

He will return sometime this evening
Bert has prepared a special dinner
Wilbur arrives just in time
And the meal is really a winner

Bert makes his favorite special sauce
He learned this one from our mother
It has pork, sausage, meatballs and cloves
It lifts my heart that he is up to it, my dear brother

The dinner is a smashing success
And we all enjoy each and every bite
We put away the meager leftovers
To savor for another night

We watch some TV and head off to bed
I'm still feeling low and depressed
I have so much to say to Wilbur
But I know he is tired and needs rest

And so we chat for just a little while
Before he is nodding off to sleep
There is nothing really important to say
And so the words to myself I keep

Tomorrow is another day
And Wilbur is up quite early again
He has a morning meeting to attend
So I will wait until after then

I'm feeling like life is passing me by
And my inspiration is waning away
I think it's my fault but don't know why
I want to keep these feelings at bay

August 19th

Bert has an appointment with the specialist today
This is good as it makes us go out
Bert is not feeling especially well
He is still having trouble with gout

The Doctor seems pre-occupied
And Bert asks for help with the catheter
He finally suggests a smaller size
Hopefully this will make things easier

And so we set out on our quest
To see which medical supply will have it
I call and find out they will have to special order
Nobody seems to regularly carry it

The order comes in and it is not correct
The supplier has substituted another
I cannot believe this simple request
Has caused so much pain for my brother

We finally reach the right pharmacy
And Wilbur takes Bert out to the store
Thank goodness they have exactly the right thing
And Bert will be much less sore

I seem to take his pain on as my own
I have enough every day
I want to let go and not be afraid
I really need to relax and pray

August 20th

It is Friday—oh goody Fosamax day
This time my stomach reacts badly
I feel nauseous the entire day long
And for myself I feel so sadly

What a sap I think, just buck up and bear it
That is my usual position
But today I am unable to muster up
I have a terrible disposition

What ever is the matter with me these days?
I should feel sunny and bright
Bert is improving every day
I want to see a miracle in sight

I need to accept these ups and downs
But I rally so hard against them
I feel so ashamed to complain myself
I feel guilty that Bert is the one

The cancer is his and clearly not mine
My diseases seem small in comparison
I fight so hard not to reveal
The pain that I'm constantly in

Please help me dear God somehow to know
Not to deny myself which makes things worse
I know this is truly silly behavior
But I don't want to feel so cursed

August 21st

Today is Saturday and the weather is lousy
It is thunder storming and raining so heavy
Wilbur and Bert go out to the store
I stay inside safe, warm and cozy

I watch some TV, the Olympics today
But I'm not really interested at all
My joints are achy my heart is heavy
And I'm not feeling well at all

I know it's the weather playing havoc
The barometer must be very low
For when it falls my joints all swell
I am a walking weatherman's show

Hopefully this will pass during the night
And tomorrow will be sunny and bright
We will be going to Alayne's house for dinner
And I want everything to be right

As if I'm the one who is in control
How absurd of me to have this opinion
I know very well I am merely a speck
I wish I could act within reason

August 22nd

Dinner is a success as well as the visit
The boys are a delight to all
They are quite well behaved and beyond that
They have quite a bit to share with us all

Alayne has scrap-booked their recent trips
And has done quite a beautiful job
We hope that when she goes through our pictures
She will be just as thrilled and absorbed

We enjoy our stay and then we must go
Wilbur wants to get the lawn mowed
For he will be leaving early tomorrow
Back to New York City he goes

He gets his chores done and packs his clothes
And we head up to watch some TV
He is watching the Olympic games
And I am lost in a good read

Soon it is time to go up to bed
And he falls asleep quite fast
He awakens me—I'm having a nightmare
I'm talking, crying and begin to gasp

I'm dreaming of our old house in New York
Someone is breaking in the house
My mother is screaming out for help
And someone has covered my mouth

I'm feeling helpless and very scared
I have trouble falling back to sleep
It all seems so real it is hard to tell
It's like a secret so dark and deep

August 23rd

I awake after Wilbur has gone for the day
And sleepily I come down the stairs
Bert is already up and having coffee
I am remembering the nightmares

I ask him if he ever remembers such an event
And he answers that he can't remember
Now I wonder if this is symbolic in some way
Of some event I don't want to remember

My mind returns to the time long ago
When I was the victim of the assault
I was forbidden to tell anyone of
The terror that was not my fault

Perhaps I am brooding over this time
I thought it was addressed and over
Or maybe it's the feeling of helplessness
And that I really have no power

Please dear God restore my good sense
To accept whatever you send
And let myself off the hook
For things I cannot mend

August 24th

I stayed up very late last night
Afraid to fall asleep
I did not want the nightmares again
Inside my head to creep

I sleep in late and this is good
I feel much better today
Today is Tuesday and aerobics again
Hopefully I can attend and stay

I still have some of the blues leftover
My brain is beaten up still
I want so badly to feel better
I wish it were a matter of will

Wilbur says I have a will of steel
If only that were really true
I would feel that I had some control
And dispose of these feelings so blue

I will speak with Diane tomorrow again
And share my thoughts with her
I know she will shed some light on this
And I'll be able to feel much better

August 25th

I went to aerobics class last night
Holding back tears all the way
My spirit was in another place
And I wasn't ready to play

Needless to say I did not do well
I stumbled around on the floor
And felt very weak in body and spirit
As I slowly left out the door

I spoke with Cindy a little bit
And she offered some good ideas
Mainly to give myself a break
All the way home I cried tears

When I met with Diane today
She told me I had the right to complain
And not to hold everything inside myself
It is detrimental to my brain

I broke down in her office a couple of times
She thinks that I'm clearly depressed
Because of the recent bout with Fibromyalgia
That has left me so tired and distressed

Later in the day I receive a call
From Jean in my former office
She asks my advice and I speak with her
She has cheered me up and lifted the abyss

Graham is here for the next few days
What a delightful young boy he is
He reads, fishes and is very smart
As a nine-year-old he shares his wishes

We have a great dinner and get ready for bed
He opts to sleep up in the loft
I tell him that he will have cat company
And he is pleased to have Sarah & Ella both

August 26th

Today I get up and go see Doug
My favorite hairdresser I've ever been to
He tells me that cutting my hair these days
Is more like shearing a hedge on cue

My hair has gotten so thick that now
I think it protects my thick head
I sincerely wish I had more energy
Instead of feeling like the dead

Today I mailed a card to Kathy
Telling her that I'm deeply wounded
I expect that she will not be surprised
We have not spent time together this summer

Later today Miss Debbie called me
To inform me that tap class will begin
She missed me last year and only had three
The class is back to Wednesday again

I am very grateful to hear this news
I need to reach out and have fun
I can't wait to see all the classmates again
To once again dance, tap and jump

I go to class tonight feeling better
I have a new frame of mind
I seem to have unloaded so much pain
And feel more gentle and kind

Thank you dear God for this happy day
Amongst the blue days I've had
It is so very good for me to feel
Happy again and not too sad

August 27th

Graham is up early, too early for me
But Wilbur gets up with him to play
And then comes upstairs to wake me up
For a breakfast of blueberry pancakes

I come down the stairs tired and sore
My muscles got a hard workout
Last night at class I pushed myself
And felt so good I could almost shout

Today I am going for a hot oil massage
What a relaxing treat it will be
I so seldom take the time for myself
And today will be just for me

Alayne is coming this afternoon
To pick up Graham and take him home
It has been such a joy to have him here
I am amazed at how much he has grown

He is really quite an intelligent boy
Wilbur has taught him to cast his line
And Bert has taught him a new computer game
That he will surely master in time

So thank you God for another good day
I so like when they turn out this well
I realize that I must push and reach out
If I'm ever to break this bad spell

August 28th

Last night we went out to listen to music
Nick and Nancy were playing
We took Uncle Bert out with us to hear
Good music is so warm it's like praying

So today I sleep in late again
My energy spent the last few days
I'm down to 113 pounds again
And can't get the scale up to stay

I suppose that is why I'm feeling tired
And also why my ribs are on fire
If only the injection of energy
Would last and not leave me tired

The twins up the street are having a party
To celebrate their 16th birthday
We are giving them money to spend
Since they are different in every way

The party was nice at the fire hall
Everyone had a great time
The theme was very festive indeed
And the food was quite divine

It's the end of another exciting week
And I'm happy to be alive
The days have been tiring and fun
Mixed with feeling good and being tired

August 29th

It is Sunday and again I sleep in late
My energy level is at minus ten
Where oh where has it disappeared
And why can't I find it again?

I get up and have a bite to eat
And read the newspaper a little
But then it is back to bed I go
And sleep away the day to the middle

Wilbur makes dinner but I am not hungry
I eat because I need the strength
I stay up and watch a little TV
And then head back to bed once again

I feel laden down as if with weights
Which prevent me from moving around
I wonder what this is all about
And hope that I can rebound

I cannot believe how tired I am
And how easily I fall asleep
What I need now is some energy
Some bounce to my step I can keep

August 30th

Today begins quite normally
I get up and have something to eat
But soon I find myself crying again
My body is consumed with grief

I go for a walk to sort things out
And find that I let off some steam
I come home and launder the bed linens
Feeling that I can at least clean

It is really myself I want to purge
The feelings that I no longer matter
There is so much pain surrounding me
It's no wonder I feel so scattered

I go up and talk with Annie for a bit
And ask her for some good advice
She comforts me and listens closely
And tells me to think things through twice

She shares some personal things with me
Which give me reason to pause
She encourages me to see Fr. Tucker
He will definitely hear my cause

Thank you God for directing me
To the exact best place to go
For in so doing we both got to share
And pray to You up above

August 31st

It is the ending of summer we never had
I hope the warm weather continues
It will take another four weeks to wait
To see if our variance is approved

Bert has developed a case of Shingles
And we must go to the Doctor today
I hope she provides some fast relief
He cannot continue on this way

Between the cancer and urinary tract
There is not too much more he can take
The added pain of the Shingles is
Enough to make anyone break

It is painful to watch my big brother cry
I want to take away some of his pain
I know that this is unreasonable
But it breaks my heart just the same

We have learned the lesson to love each other
And to share what we have to give
I don't understand God's message here
We just want to live and let live

Please help us dear God to understand
And to deal with what we have been given
I know that if You lead us to it
You will lead us out through it again

September 1st

It is Wednesday, the 1st of September
The middle of a harrowing week
I take Bert to the Doctor to see
If it is Shingles making him so weak

She checks him over and gives her advice
She does not believe Shingles is the cause
Of the crazy rash on the back of his leg
It is something else of which she is not sure

So home we come and Bert takes a rest
A much needed rest indeed
I too am tired and want to cry
But I have to hold back my tears

I hide my feelings from my brother
He has enough on his mind
I feel so badly I can feel his pain
Although it clearly is not mine

So once again I am turning to God
To make some sense out of this mess
I do have faith and I trust and believe
That He will guide us through this test

September 2nd

I rest for a good part of the day
Bert is finally feeling better
I receive a call from Jean at work
She is bored from writing collection letters

She manages to lift my spirits a bit
She can tell that I've not been well
In fact I find myself crying to her
There are many tears left in the well

It is aerobics night and I feel free
To go and work out my troubled mind
The women are very gracious to me
I push hard to leave the troubles behind

We all to ten pushups just for Bert
It is easy when there is just cause
We do ten for ourselves and then I rest
Before I am able to do ten more

I have worked so hard I don't want to leave
If only I were able to heal
Bert's Cancer and my Fibromyalgia
I could work out until next year

I come home and take a nice warm shower
My body is really tired and spent
I have pushed and worked so very hard
Tonight was the last day on the floor of cement

Next week we move back to the gym
Where the floor is much more forgiving
I'll be so excited to see how well
The workouts have improved my being

September 3rd

I wake up early and think of my Dad
He passed away twenty years ago this day
I drive to church and say a prayer
And speak with Fr. Tucker along the way

I read him the introduction to my book
He says I am hard working and strong
I find it funny that I feel so fragile
And that somehow I don't belong

He tells me to give myself a break
That it takes a lot of time to heal the strife
I ask him just how long does it take?
He answers "the rest of your life"

At first I think he must be joking
And then he gets right in my face
And tells me I must slow down and listen
To God's words of healing and grace

I leave feeling humbled and drive myself home
Thinking all along the way
There must be a way to hasten recovery
It is then that I pause and pray

September 4th

After yesterday's meeting with Fr. Tucker
I came home and took a nap
And then went for my meeting with Diane
My brain is now totally zapped

She reiterates just what Fr. Tucker said
It is if she were present herself
Now I'm hearing the same message twice
And know I must take care of myself

I must distance Bert's pain from my own
I can empathize with him and pray
But now I know that no matter what
I cannot take his pain away

It is his to bear for whatever reason
And I have enough of my own
I must let go of the feelings that I have
That I can fix everything on my own

I am no use to him or to my husband
If I do not take care of myself first
This is a very humbling fact of life
I'm so used to putting myself last

September 5th

I am sleeping in late again today
We went to Lynne and Dave's for supper
It was spur of the moment and so much fun
We decide we must do this more often

It is Labor Day Weekend and we have no plans
I am truly grateful for this
I can lie around and do nothing at all
If that is what I choose or wish

Bert and I decide to go for a walk
Wilbur is outside cutting the grass
We take our time and walk leisurely
Enjoying each others company at last

We are both tired when we finally reach home
The sun was too much for us to bear
I head upstairs to take a shower
While Bert relaxes in his chair

We have a good dinner and watch some TV
We have all done what we each wanted
How wonderful it is to have these days
To remember and upon which to ponder

September 6th

I wake up and realize today is the day
When re-runs of Law and Order
Will play all day long on the TV
I hog the remote and take over

No-one else cares, they are otherwise busy
And I think this day has been made just for me
And so I do a few loads of laundry
And then head upstairs to watch the TV

It is said that too much watching TV
Can turn your brain into mush
But I have learned so much from this series
It inspires my legal brain to seek justice

Perhaps when I'm well I will volunteer
A day or two of my time per week
To lend myself to legal aide
For those who have no voice to speak

I catch every detail and nuance of the show
So that I can clearly remember
Just how difficult the justice system is
And that I once was considered a member

As merely a Para-legal of course
My focus was in commercial real estate
But I did have the chance occasionally to work
In other areas of interest that I cared to take

September 7th

Tonight is the time we move back to the gym
I am so excited I can hardly wait
I am working so hard to better myself
That sometimes my muscles do ache

But the gym floor is softer on my feet
And on my entire body as well
I feel the energy building inside me now
It will be fun just to see and tell

If there really is a difference to mark
How difficult the exercises are
For tomorrow night I will return to tap
And I feel like I'm reaching for a star

I'm finally beginning to see some light
At the end of this long dark tunnel
I have been traveling in for quite some time
There is finally in sight some fun

Oh how I look forward to having some fun
And not have to pay the price in pain
I truly hope that is what's in store
Some real sunshine instead of rain

September 8th

I am up and about very early today
My stomach is growling with hunger
I head downstairs to have some breakfast
And take extra time to ponder

Last night's workout was very intense
I added a riser to my step
Which doubled the intensity of every move
And I was totally drenched in sweat

I felt very proud of myself indeed
It has been a very long time
Since I worked that hard in any class
This time the victory was mine

Tonight I begin tapping again
It has been over one year's time
Since I felt good enough to trust myself
To start tapping and have a good time

I think that I am strong enough to begin
Something that I think is really fun
The aerobics class is very hard work
But tap is like dancing in the sun

Thank you God for this chance again
To go out and tap with my friends
I know that I have been building strength
And I can't wait to use it again

September 9th

I am tired today and quite exhausted
Last night's workout was very hard
But I am looking forward to later
When I get to fill my dancing card

I leave a bit early and get totally lost
Before I call the studio to find out
Just where the hell they are on Route 4
I'm in the car and totally freaking out

I finally slow down and find the place
It is not very well marked at all
But once I find it I go inside
And say hello to fellow dancers all

The class is much tougher than I think
And before long I am totally drenched
I've forgotten what a workout this is
And am glad I brought water to drink

I come home take a shower and head off to bed
This is one worn out sleepy old gal
I feel the Fibromyalgia creeping in
But I refuse to acknowledge it somehow

I just need some sleep and I'll be fine
How often have I spoken these words?
I fall asleep but somehow I know
Tomorrow I will eat these very same words

September 10th

Today I awake in full-blown pain
I am mad and frustrated again
Bert has a Dr. appointment today
And Wilbur will be the one to take him

I feel so let down but I don't give in
I refuse to take pain meds all day long
Because I want to attend class tonight
What a fool I can be and so wrong

At about 5:30 in the afternoon
It is quite apparent to me
That I will be going nowhere tonight
Except to bed with some tea

I call Cindy and leave a message for her
Telling her I'm fighting with all my might
But that I probably will not be there
With all my friends later tonight

I take this defeat along with my meds
And feel so lousy I can't explain
My ribs are on fire and so is my back
I can no longer tolerate the pain

September 11th

What a horrible day for our entire country
And a terrible one for me as well
I am resting in bed all day long
And the meds make me feel like hell

This is the worst attack I've had
Sine this horrible disease began
I try to lay still and remain calm
But I am not able to complain

I want some help—I need some help
But I simply don't know how to ask
Wilbur is out working in the barn
And Bert is certainly not up to the task

How strange is this for us both to be sick
At precisely the same exact time
Neither of us can do for the other
Wilbur must take over and he doesn't mind

I guess this is one of those blessings that come
Neatly wrapped up and disguised
I am not feeling thankful at all
In fact I'm feeling quite surprised

Just why would God choose this time
For us both to feel so sick and lousy?
We are both in pain and nauseous besides
We are feeling so weak and drowsy

September 12th

Another day totally wasted
Sleeping and being in pain
This is going on too long
I need some relief from the strain

Wilbur is leaving for New York City
Later sometime this afternoon
Bert and I will have to make do
Wilbur will make supper soon

And then it will be back up to bed
I can't seem to hold up my head
I have a bout in the bathroom again
I think I'm feeling somewhat dead

I cannot believe this is lasting so long
I am unable to stay awake
I really want to feel better again
I wonder how long it will take

I think about calling friends on the phone
But decide to lay still and to pray
Please dear God send us some help
We all need relief right away

September 13th

I wake up and think I could not feel worse
And then I get out of the bed
I'm dizzy, nauseous and very weak
And there's a terrible pain in my head

I feel like I have a big hangover
However with nothing to drink
I push myself to make breakfast for us
French toast for Bert and I'm now on the brink

I can barely stand up at the stove
And think I'm going to throw-up
So I sit down in between cooking
And finally Bert rouses himself up

Neither of us is very hungry at all
But I know we'll feel better once we eat
So we push ourselves to the table
And are both grateful for the treat

I take a short rest and then get up
Feeling some energy once again
I remove the sheets from the beds
And round up the rest of the laundry

I make the beds up with clean fresh sheets
There is such healing in this task
I know that later sometime this evening
We will all go to bed and bask

I hope this energy lasts for the day
But I plan to pace myself well
I don't want to over-do again
And end up in the place called hell

September 14th

It is Tuesday and I'm still feeling small
I wish this tiredness would fade away
Some energy is what is really needed
And then I could simply fly away

I am not strong enough yet to go to class
Although it is what I want to do
Move these muscles around a bit
And feel stronger through and through

But it's not in the plan and so I accept
Not very graciously I'm afraid
That my job today is to stay home and rest
While the others go out and play

This disease is consuming me bit by bit
I get smaller each time I weigh
I must find a way to beat this thing
I should stop complaining and pray

So that is what I will do today
Thank God for all of my blessings
They are easy to count and easy to see
When I do I start to feel better?

September 15th

Wednesday is here and I'm smiling again
I know that if I am very careful
I will be able to attend tap class tonight
And this class is truly wonderful

What great fun and spirit we share
Frankie and all of us women
He makes us laugh at ourselves and then
We are all tapping together in rhythm

The day passes by not quickly enough
I am anxious to go out and have fun
I need to laugh and play like a child
Because Bert's illness is so glum

Between the two of us it is very hard
To keep the faith and to smile
We both need a lot more humor in life
Even if it's just for awhile

I'm working very hard to build my strength
To have enough to carry us both through
But I must be careful to take care of myself
Or there will be no strength left for us two

I spend much more time today in prayer
Thank you dear God for this special day
I try to keep things in perspective
Please send more of them our way

September 16th

This morning I go for my usual trim
And Doug is charming and delightful
He thanks me for brightening up his day
It is actually him who makes me feel special

A new hair-cut always does the trick
I feel spunky and full of life
Wilbur takes Bert to the hospital today
And when they return I see strife

Bert is extremely tired today
And is running a slight temperature
Between the chemo and antibiotics
He looks and feels like hell for sure

I am frightened to see him look so bad
I go to class to clear my head
I cry on the way and back home too
I work so hard I can't wait to get into bed

I am truly afraid and cry as I pray
Wilbur comforts me and holds me close
I want my brother to feel alive
And not look and feel so morose

Sleep finally comes and I am grateful
To have some relief from this pain
Tomorrow will come and be brighter I'm sure
And we'll go through this process again

September 17th

The results of hurricane Ivan are on the way
I can feel the barometer dropping fast
I take Bert to the hospital again
For his treatment of antibiotic blast

The process takes about half an hour
And we meet with his treatment friend
Her name is Ruth and she is delightful
She has truly become a Godsend

They meet every day at eleven o'clock
To receive their antibiotic potion
She has a recurrence of Lyme Disease
While Bert has a urinary infection

The staff is wonderful to my surprise
They seem to put everyone at ease
This must really be a difficult task
For everyone is not easy to please

I remember to pray for each of them
The jobs they hold are not easy
But they smile and greet each new day
And make us all feel carefree and breezy

September 18th

The rain is falling and the wind is howling
I cannot seem to move out of bed
I test my joints one at a time
They are all swollen and so is my head

Wilbur takes Bert for his treatment today
I am in too much pain to move
I gradually get up and take my meds
Then it is back to bed I choose

The barometer must have fallen so very low
My body feels like everything is broken
It takes both Vioxx and pain medication
To calm down the pain in slow motion

The day is dreadful and much too long
I want the weather to break soon
We promised to take Bert to the church picnic
Which will be held tomorrow afternoon

I read for a while and watch some TV
And then fall asleep thank heaven
I awake still in pain and wonder when
I will feel some relief from this burden

It is nighttime now and time for bed
I am grateful to feel some relief
I thank God for my blessings today
For I truly and sincerely do believe

September 19th

It is Sunday morning and the weather has cleared
It is chilly and still quite windy outside
I take Bert to the hospital again
And when we return home we decide

To go to the picnic and see our friends
Where Bert is the center of attention
We eat the usual picnic fare
And try to stay warm in the pavilion

It was so good for Bert to be out and about
And to chat with his many, many friends
I felt to proud to be his sister
And be able to share this day with him

Someone has put together a beautiful book
Of the party previously held in Bert's honor
We bring it home and are filled with tears
It is quite a tribute through the pages we wander

We come home and Bert is so grateful he cries
He is happy to have been able to attend
I am thankful that we all could go
And remember to thank God at the end

September 20th

We begin our day at the hospital again
We are getting to be known as "the happy group"
Ruth and Bert and I chat together
Along with the nurses who are a very good troupe

We laugh and pass the time together
It seems we are done in no time at all
I know we have formed a special friendship
And we must remember to call

There was a great article about Dr. DeVanney
In the Hartford Courant this morning
So we stop on our way home to pick up a copy
To read and keep for our journalizing

We are all a bit tired from yesterday
But no one is complaining
We had such a good time all together
And were glad that it wasn't raining

It's the night to stay up and watch TV
All the re-runs of "Law and Order"
It has become one of my favorite shows
Along with "Oprah" the best TV has to offer

I feel good and cook dinner tonight
This is really a very rare occasion
We have baked ham, noodles and broccoli rabe
And Wilbur thinks he's on vacation

September 21st

I baked cinnamon biscotti last evening
Along with some pumpkin gingerbread
I bring some in to the hospital nurses
And a sample for Ruth in her bed

She was late this morning and did not arrive
Until later in the afternoon—what a surprise
She called me to thank me for making her day
I told her it was easy she is such a delight

I think we'll all probably keep in touch
She has been such good company for us all
I must remember to ask her where
She goes to spend time in Florida in the fall

I'm able to attend class tonight
And work extra hard to catch up
I think I actually worked too hard
I drink my water by the cup

None-the-less I am glad for the day
And the beautiful weather we have
It is so easy to take for granted
When the sky is blue and the barometer high

I remember to thank God for this day
And ask for a few more like this one
It has lifted our spirits so very high
We want to greet and hug everyone

September 22nd

It is my daughter Alayne's birthday
And I phone and sing her a song
I know that she is working very hard
At St. Anthony's school where she belongs

They are lucky to have her in their employ
To handle the special Ed children
She has a lot of patience indeed
And loves helping them to learn

I awake feeling a little like disaster
I know I pushed too far last night
My ribs are sore and I stay in bed
A time to fight the good fight

Bert goes to the hospital by himself
He is proud to be able to do this
I am clearly disappointed in myself
I have nothing left over to give

So later this afternoon we drive
To Bristol and visit the birthday girl
She loves her presents and is already planning
Her outfit to wear tomorrow with a whirl

We visit for a while and Graham plays for us
The flute he picked up just last week
He has mastered some notes and gets clear sounds
When he practices he will be just great

We drive home and stop for our Wednesday fare
Of Chinese take out for dinner
I have chosen to skip tap class
This decision is truly a winner

I thank God in prayer for the beautiful day
And ask Him to take away some of the pain
My ribs hurt so much it is difficult to breathe
And I've learned when to call it a day

September 22nd

To My Dear Daughter Alayne

You began life as a beautiful baby girl
With dark curls and sparkling blue eyes
The child people stopped to look at
In complete wonder and surprise

You grew into a lovely young woman
Artistic and very talented you were
For when you danced Ballet on Pointe
The audience was captured they did not stir

And now you are a beautiful wife and mother
Blessed with two young handsome sons
They are wonderful boys and talented too
I look forward to what is to come

You create magical picture books
To cherish those special memories
Your creative talents are still in place
There are many people you please

And now you are working with Special Ed children
How fortunate they are to have you
As teacher, leader and a source of guidance
I am so very proud of you

As a daughter and friend I could not ask
For a better person than you
God has truly blessed me greatly
When He looked down and sent me you

September 23rd

Although I went to bed earlier than usual
I did not sleep very well last night
Wilbur was snoring and it was hot
So I got up instead to write

I think that over the past few weeks
I've not shown my true emotions
I find that my body and mind are weak
I must find energy in some magic potion

I know what to do and fault myself
For neglecting to take care of what should be
It seems so easy to be consumed
By the frantic life surrounding me

I promise this day to make certain decisions
That will truly benefit my being
Taking my vitamins along with my meds
And trying to ignore the martyr thing

I plan to attend aerobics class tonight
But to take it easy with myself
To do what I can without pushing too far
And ask God to help be my strength

September 24th

It is Friday morning and I am in pain
But I'll soon be going for a hot oil massage
I find myself melting into the table
And use the hour to pray and thank God

The therapist is gifted, talented and uses her sense
She kneads my body and works out the kinks
To find the trouble spots, which prove to be many
And when she hits nerves I don't even blink

This time is so sacred and special to me
And also to the therapist who prays while she works
It is a spiritual ritual for both of us
I leave pain free and nothing seems to hurt

I come home and rest and drink lots of water
This feeling does not last through the day
I take advantage of the short time I have
And am thankful for it and remember to pray

We are going to take my brother out tonight
He offers to buy dinner it is his turn to treat
And listen to music that brings him such joy
It makes me happy he is so sweet

September 25th

It is the weekend and Bert must go
Back to the hospital for his daily trip
To receive antibiotics to cure the infection
Through the PICC line and daily drip

He is getting tired of this daily routine
Who wouldn't feel the same way?
But yet we muster up and drive again
We must do this every single day

They test his urine and run the culture
It will take at least 48 hours
So in the interim he still must go
Have the PICC line flushed every 24 hours

We come home and it is rainy and cold
The house is damp and too chilly
So we turn on the furnace to warm ourselves
For the season this is way too early

But cold and stiff joints hurt too much
To ignore how we all are feeling
We head off to bed to take our naps
With our heads rocking and reeling

We come down and have dinner to share
Our time to be all together
We will stay this way no matter what
The season or the weather

Thank God for the day for us to share
Our love for one another
Sister and husband are happy to have
Life here with my brother

September 26th

Another peaceful day to share
I read and Bert slumbers
Wilbur is out working in the barn
On a rocking horse for a friend's granddaughter

This is a day of rest indeed
We each do what we want
Nobody has an agenda today
We are free to go for a jaunt

Bert and I go for a little walk
He is nervous about the coming week
He is scheduled for a MRI tomorrow
He is scared but does not speak

This one will be of his lumbar spine
And compared to the one 6 months ago
He still must go and have the PICC line flushed
There are so many things to do

We return home and he is wiped out
He still has much more testing to be done
I am afraid for him but try to be strong
This is anything for him but fun

I go to bed weeping and try to sleep
But sleep is eluding me most nights
I am worried to death that he might die
And I look and feel like a fright

Wilbur comes up to comfort me
But I hold on fast to my fears
It is nobody's fault I understand
But I can no longer hold back the tears

September 27th

This morning we all rise very early
Wilbur is off to New York City
Bert and I arrive at the hospital
And I go down the hall to sit

The MRI takes about an hour
Which seems like half of a day
I am waiting impatiently for him
But somehow I manage to pray

We will not know the results until next week
When Dr. DeVanney returns to work
His wife has just had a brand new baby
And he is helping out after the birth

Bert finally emerges and I give him a hug
We now must go up to the second floor
To have the PICC line flushed again
Dear God what else and how much more?

We finally leave and head for home
Now I am getting nervous myself
For I have a Doctor appointment tomorrow
She will not be happy with the status of my health

I take a nap and so does Bert
I curl up with Sarah the cat
She knows that I am not feeling well
As she lays down and purrs in my lap

We get up and make a very small dinner
Wilbur calls to check on us
We both speak to him on the phone
There is too much to really discuss

I go upstairs to watch some TV
Reruns of "Law and Order"
I love this show I think it's because
It gives my legal mind food for fodder

September 28th

Another day to rise early again
I drop Bert off at the hospital
While I go to my Dr. visit
Which turns out to be quite horrible

She tells me I don't look very well
And I explain what is going on
She knows that I'm too emotional
I cry and she gently calms me down

She listens very carefully when I speak
And she clearly has true empathy
But she tells me I must improve myself
Before I can lend any sympathy

I tell her the Vioxx is not working at all
And she changes my drug to Bextra
She urges me to see my counselor
And I tell her I will see her tomorrow

I go back to the hospital to pick up Bert
He can tell that I've been crying
He asks me what's wrong but I cannot talk
Instead I make up some lying

We are done with Doctors for the day
And head back home to the farm
This is one day I'm glad is over
It's been like setting off an alarm

September 29th

Today it's a trip to the hospital again
This time is for Bert's Bone Scan
He thinks he can drive by himself
And I let him because he can

He gets out earlier than he thought
And runs some errands he has
I'm amazed that he truly has the courage
He stops to fill up his car with gas

I have an appointment with the therapist
And Wilbur joins me this time
I fall apart in no time at all
Diane must now find a new line

She promises to call Dr. Oltikar
And decide what to do about my meds
I will meet with her later this week
And we'll talk about what has been said

I know I'm a mess and still in pain
I want so much to be in control
God clearly has other plans for me
I feel like an empty old bowl

Yearning to be filled with lots of good things
Like food and pretty decorations
I fail to even apply my makeup
Which would certainly help my facial expressions

We head back home and I remain quiet
It is unusual for me to be so somber
Wilbur comments on our way home
I cry and tell him I must ponder

September 30th

Today it is off to the hospital again
This time for another MRI
I can't believe how much trauma there is
In only one short week's time

I take Bert in and wait once more
This time in silence I pray
There are many folks in the waiting room
And I wonder how long they will stay

I find myself praying for them all
For each has their very own burden
It takes up my time as I look at each face
Some are filled with worry, some laden

Pretty soon Bert appears and he looks good
I know he is worried about the results
I must admit that I am scared to death
They are looking for way too much

But very soon we will have some answers
To the many questions we have
We must be patient to learn the news
And all the results done in the lab

I thank God for one more day to spend
With my loving brother so dear
I continue to pray and pray some more
Please God I hope you can hear

October 1st

This morning we pack for a weekend away
Wilbur and I are definitely in need
Of some time to spend in the mountains
And we head to Vermont with great speed

We are meeting our friends Arlene & Fred
Who have taken such good care of Bert
We gifted them with this weekend away
At our very favorite Inn in Vermont

They are already there when we arrive
And are taking a walk in the woods
We greet them with hugs when they return
We are all feeling fortunate and good

We have asked a neighbor to check in on Bert
Just to give him a call on the phone
When we call home we find out however
That Deb has brought dinner to him at home

He is delighted and thinks this is great
To live in a neighborhood so warm
Since he has only been here since July
Everyone has made him feel welcome

We go up and get dressed for dinner tonight
Which we are having at the Inn
We order champagne to celebrate
All the trials through which we have been

October 2nd

Today we wake up and have breakfast together
The food and hospitality are wonderful
We make plans to travel to Woodstock today
And then decide what we'll do later on

Woodstock is a wonderful place
There are shops and a general store
I happen to enter a small toyshop
And leave with a giant bear out the door

Wilbur must carry "Jake" on his shoulders
As he makes his way to the car
Many children stop to stare
Some people take his picture from afar

We decide to go to Quechee for lunch
And find another great eating spot
We have a lunch that is so grand
We go for a walk and then another shop

We find a place named "Candle in the Wind"
They sell soy candles and many good things
Arlene is looking for just the right item
And finds it so easily she sings

We then head home back to the Inn
To rest up for dinner tonight
We go out to a familiar place
But I am not feeling all right

So we drive back to the Inn and say goodnight
I draw myself a hot bath in the tub
And soak for a very long, long time
Hoping to ease the pain with a rub

I hop into bed and find Wilbur asleep
But sleep does not easily come
I pray in thanks for this time away
And for all those whom I love

October 3rd

Today we again have breakfast together
We enjoy our time for soon we must go
The "Juniper Hill Inn" is simply fabulous
We pack up our things to head home

Arlene & Fred will take their time
Stopping in Weston and other towns
We will; however, head straight home
I take pain pills hoping to drown

The pain that remains deep in my spine
I long to sleep in my own bed
Three hours plus spent on the road
Are too much for my sleepy little head

I doze on and off throughout the drive
I am anxious and still in pain
We stop at a rest stop on the way
And I take some pills once again

We finally arrive home in the afternoon
Bert is so happy to see us
Deb brought him dinner again last night
He thanked her for being so generous

I tell him that I am not one bit surprised
Because that is what this neighborhood is about
Helping one another when there is need
He realizes how fortunate we are no doubt

I bring him in the few things that I've bought
And he laughs at the size of the new bear
Who is wearing Wilbur's brown suede vest
It's too small for him everywhere

Bert has prepared dinner for us
A surprise, which he likes to do
We are delighted and dine together
Wilbur cleans up and I bid adieu

October 4th

Today we head off to the hospital again
This time for cleaning and draining
We know the infection is still there
Roaming around causing much pain

We are scheduled to see his Doctor tomorrow
Who will have the results of the tests
We look forward to going and hoping to find
That the results are good this would be the best

We come home leisurely and stop on the way
At the health food store in town
We need some granola for breakfast time
For the container is completely gone

We both rest up in the afternoon
Taking it easy for the day
I am still in a great deal of pain
I take pain meds and fade away

They do not last long and I am worried
Just what is this new pain from?
Then I decide it must be the mattress
Or the time in the car was too long

Wilbur has left for a fishing trip
And I am not happy with this
But he goes every fall with his 2 friends
And I find that my anger I must dismiss

He deserves some special time too
Although he is aware of my pain
Somehow I think that he can fix it
But I pray harder once again

October 5th

Today it is off to the DR's. Office
To learn the results of the tests
We speak with him for quite a long time
And he offers the options at best

The good news is that the tumor has shrunk
Substantially in it's size
But we still must consider an Oncologist
Who will offer radiation, which is wise

Bert will need to have an operation
To clean out the balloon in the bladder
If that does not work then the next option is
To sew up and remove the bubble

The Doctor is taking it one step at a time
Not wanting Bert to go through too much hell
But the infection is still present and he must decide
Which antibiotic will kill these darn cells

The urine is cultured and sensitized
To establish which antibiotic to use
He has already had three weeks of drugs
And he is feeling used and abused

Needless to say I am not happy
I want him to get better now
The antibiotics make him feel tired
And he is more susceptible somehow

And so I resort to prayer again
And return to class tonight
It feels good to move my body around
And Cindy keeps it easy and light

October 6th

Today we are blessed with a lovely visit
From our close friends Rosie and Stan
They have traveled the long way from Manchester
Just to see how we are and how things stand

It is a joyful visit and we give them updates
As to both my brother and me
Our situations seem gloomy at best
But we all look forward hopefully

The addition was finally approved last night
And the digging will begin next week
This has picked up everyone's spirit
And provided something solid to keep

I am depressed and don't understand why
But it is truly an awful feeling
I am suffering with bouts of pain and loss
And find that my mind is reeling

I will see Diane later this week
Perhaps she can piece it together
I think it is partially the time of year
I left work and partially the weather

It has been extremely cold so early
We have been forced to turn on the heat
For when I get chilled the pain is worse
And I pray that this pain I can beat

October 7th

Today I see Doug for a color and cut
I so enjoy this time out with him
It is a respite from all the troubles
Which are usually all quite grim

He asks about my health and then
He asks about my brother's condition
We talk while he works so effortlessly
And I am comforted and laugh with him

He makes me feel like a kid again
He tells me I am his cutie
I'm not quite sure who benefits the most
Myself or him performing his duty

I leave the shop smiling at last
And head home to rest for a while
It was certainly beneficial for me to get out
And return home with a brand new smile

I feel perked up for a little bit
And this is a good thing for me
I thank God for all my blessings today
And the future ones I cannot yet see

October 8th

It is Friday and the end of the week
I am more tired than usual
But Wilbur and I decide to go out
And listen to our favorite music

He has just returned from a week of fishing
And I find myself resentful of this
So when we go out I lash out at him
I don't like my own disposition

We come home early because he feels sick
I think it's because he is mad at me
I offer to get him an Alka-Seltzer
But he refuses and totally rejects me

Now I know he is totally mad
And he falls asleep snoring loudly
My feelings are hurt and I cannot sleep
I am offended and not feeling too proudly

I go up to the loft to get some peace
But find that I can still hear him snoring
I go up and close the door to the bedroom
At times I wish life were more boring

I pray to God to quiet my heart
Which is pounding so loud in my chest
I am desperate for sleep and peace of mind
Please help me God, You know what's best

October 9th

The weekend at last and I am still tired
I meet with the therapist and I am teary
We speak at great length about my meds
She wants to change them I'm so weary

I agree to the plan, which will take some time
To slowly achieve the change and ensure
I must decrease one and then add a new drug
I need to feel better that is for sure

Tonight we are playing our Trivia game
With our friends we see once a month
I don't really feel much like going out
But I feel obligated to see our happy bunch

I am glad when we get there and I can see
That Donna's hair is growing again
Two of the women are treating for breast cancer
And I feel guilty to discuss my pain

But yet it is real and I am stifling myself
Because I don't want to talk
So instead we play and eat goodies
I feel the need to go for a walk

We play two games and the men win both
The women are exhausted and feel dumb
I was never really into the game
And on the way home I feel numb

I pray once again to God up above
To grace me with whatever I need
I know that my heart is quite heavy
I have not been kind in thought or deed

October 10th

It is Sunday morning and the air is cool
Both outside and in my heart
Bert heads off to the hospital again
And Wilbur and I have a chance to talk

We both speak honestly about what is bothering us
And find it a great relief, even in tears
To finally get to unload my feelings to him
And to also get to listen to his fears

We need to do this much more often
But his traveling prevents this from happening
We vow to take the necessary time
To keep up with how each of us is feeling

I am comforted now and feel much better
And Wilbur is feeling the same
We have so much on our plates
But no one is really to blame

We just must slow down and make time for us
Which is difficult to do every night
But soon the addition will be complete
And we are blessed to have this in sight

So thank you dear Lord for our time today
A special time for us indeed
And help me to be more open to You
When You answer my prayers in need

October 11th

Today I head off to see Doc Spiegel
I know he will be pleased with my weight gain
For now I've gone from one hundred nine
To a grand high of one hundred seventeen

But when I get there I break down in tears
And share with him what's going on
He listens to me very patiently
And tells me that I must move on

I share with him how discouraged I feel
That I am disgusted and very blue
He understands quite well just how I feel
And paints a new picture for me to view

It's been a long day and when we are through
I stop to browse at the local bookstore
To find some uplifting reading for myself
I linger and purchase three books more

I get home quite late; it's just Bert and me
For Wilbur is working in New York
I make dinner for both of us easily
And find that it's really not a chore

So thank you dear God for sending me
Just exactly in the right direction
You always know what it is I need
And lead me to the right selections

October 12th

Today is Bert's pre-op testing day
He will be at the hospital for a while
And when he returns he is very tired
He feels like he has walked a mile

We talk for a bit, I know he is scared
Of what tomorrow will bring
Surgery and pain and an overnight stay
He is not looking forward to this thing

We fiddle around the house to fill
The nervous time to work through
I am trying with all my might
To be supportive and not feel blue

But I am not feeling my best these days
And depression and pain are the cause
I must try to maintain a cheerful outlook
And not give Bert reason to pause

I know in my heart that I am weak
It is difficult to pretend to be strong
But that is exactly what I do
And I fake it the entire day-long

Thank you dear God for picking me up
When I want to lie down and cry
You keep me busy with little things
I know You know how hard I try

October 13th

We arrive at the hospital at 8:30 AM
The surgery is scheduled for ten
I go with Bert to the pre-op room
We are both nervous and wait again

The surgery is late when they finally call
It is now almost eleven twenty
I kiss him and remind him how much I care
And go out to the waiting room, which is empty

I lie down and try to take a nap
It is useless for I cannot sleep
Finally the Doctor comes over to me
Shows me pictures and says go home and sleep

The surgery itself was a great success
And I return to visit later in the day
There are problems with many blood clots forming
And the staff works hard to take them away

Bert is weak and I am tired
This entire process is overload
He is sobbing and in much pain
It is very difficult for me to hold

I kiss him goodnight and wish him some rest
For I know that he is truly exhausted
Things do not go well during the night
His blood clots keep right on forming

October 14th

I wake up when Bert phones me
He has had a terrible night
They have given him two units of blood
I am terrified but maintain my fight

I bake some biscotti to take with me
And drop some off to the nurses
They thank me very graciously
And I go to see Bert who curses

He cries and says he wants to come home
But the Doctor has other plans
He wants to keep him for one more day
This is good as Bert has more pain

I find out that they had to remove
More than thirty clots during the night
His body is still forming them
And now he must regain his fight

I stay for a while and then come home
Where I dress for aerobics class
I know I must work off this anxiety
And aerobics is just the right place

I return home and pray and pray some more
I want Bert to be home with us
Miss Mary, his cat is frantic enough
She does not find comfort with us

And so we stroke her and talk to her
While Bert receives two more units of blood
She goes up to his room looking for him
And then snuggles under the covers

October 15th

Bert calls and wakes me up again
And says he is free to come home
I am delighted and wait for Wilbur
I know I can't handle this alone

We finally stop at the pharmacy
To pick up for Bert some new meds
Bert can barely make it up the stairs
And I help him get into his bed

He comes downstairs later in the day
And I help him drain the catheter bag
He is thankful for help but embarrassed a bit
I remind him I'm his sister what a drag

We share a laugh or two together
Brother and sister we truly have become
I tell him that parts are simply parts
If reversed he would have to succumb

We laugh and joke about this for a while
There is nothing too impossible here
It is just uncomfortable for all of us
I think we should all share a beer

We all thank God for His gentle care
He reminds me that worry is sinful
Something that Fr. Lou first told me
To pray is much more faithful

October 16th

Bert wakes up in a lot of pain
I try to help him along
But he is still passing new blood clots
And I pray for healing with a song

We will miss going to Manchester today
For a pot luck dinner which was planned
Instead I try to comfort his mind
With a few laughs we take a new stand

I am in much pain myself
But I do not share this with him
I take my meds to find relief
And calm us both down with a hymn

The weekend is not what we had in mind
We thought he would be fairly strong
But the complications after surgery
Have taken a big toll all along

I pray to God for saving his life
There seems to be too much pain
What we really need here is simple enough
A light and healing soft rain

October 17th

My brother and I are still in pain
We try to make things quite calm
For later today Wilbur will travel
To New York City again

We have a big dinner early today
And settle things up by afternoon
Wilbur leaves and we say goodbye
And we each watch TV till we snooze

I am thankful for getting through the day
Even with two out of three in serious pain
We move around slowly all day long
Our home has become almost insane

I am learning albeit very late
That I must thank God for each day
For no matter what He is there for me
And I am thankful in every way

He is there in good times and in pain
I know that there's a lesson to learn
I must concentrate and focus on good
And let Him guide me in turn

October 18th

Today is a busy day for us
We drop off boxes of coats and shoes
The Goodwill folks are happy to see us
For many people will benefit and use

We phone Dr. DeVanney with many questions
And then we call Dr. Oltikar too
She wants to see Bert tomorrow
To find out just what to do

We then head off to look at fixtures
For Bert's new kitchen and bath
We take a long time to make some choices
We ponder as we do the math

The items he chooses are expensive indeed
But we want him to have the best
He has suffered and needed far too long
We want his place to be a place of rest

We then head off to the pharmacy
Everyone knows us by sight
We chat for a while with the staff
They are all cheerful and bright

October 19th

We meet Dr. DeVanney at eight o'clock
He removes the painful catheter
Hopefully Bert will be able to void
On his own with no catheter

We come home and rest up for awhile
And then it is again time to move
We meet Dr. Oltikar promptly at two
And she recommends an Oncologist to use

She sets up an appointment for Bert to see
The Oncologist, who happens to be her friend
She is rated as one of the ten top docs
We will see her the ninth of November

Now we head home for the rest of the day
Rest is truly what we both need
Brother and sister we are really a sight
We both crash and follow God's lead

I remember to pray for everyone
Including my brother and me
The pain and trauma are simply too much
We must rise up in order just to be

Thank you dear Lord for another day
For with pain we know that we are alive
It is difficult for each of us to truly give thanks
But we do so and know this is wise

October 20th

We all sleep in quite late today
It somehow feels like a reward
We look out the window in surprise
The crew is working in the yard

I see my therapist today at noon
She says I look a bit better
I took the time to make up my face
For things we have to do later

We talk for awhile just about me
I tell her I am in great pain
Both physically and emotionally
I feel like I could slip though a drain

She gives me more meds to up the dose
In hopes that I'll get some relief
I simply sit and cry out loud
I want to be healthy without having to reach

It is time now to go to my old place of work
To pick up the last of my personal things
I visit with folks for a very short time
I am tired and just want to leave

My boss tells me how much he misses me
That there is no one to take my place
I thank him for his very kind words
I feel really blessed with grace

October 21st

We get up very early today
To take Bert again to the hospital
To the lab for a complete blood workup
And we then see our first miracle

I had previously sent a very kind letter
To the president and CEO
We take a chance to meet with him
And he ushers us in with a glow

We speak for a bit and tell him how good
His staff members treated Bert
He then becomes very spiritual
And offers Bert a card from his shirt

It is a card with the Sacred Heart
He tells Bert to wear it in his pocket
Every moment that he is awake
It seems like a perfect locket

We then speak about my draft book
He is interested at once in the topic of pain
He tells me to bring him a completed draft
He will personally deliver it to a celebrity at hand

October 22nd

I arise quite late once again
This is a very good thing for me
I am unfortunately in a lot of pain
And am thankful for the time just to be

This evening I will go to my daughter's house
To attend a terrific craft show
To purchase a number of things for others
And then it will be time to go

Alayne introduces me to all her friends
She is now quite proud of me
She never before would admit this fact
I am again grateful just to be

I admire the people she has chosen as friends
There are many women in this group
Women from soccer or the library
Then there are the teachers they're a hoot

Alayne has carved a niche for herself
With many good people to share
As I leave I thank God for her
And say a special prayer

October 23rd

Today I awake in much pain again
I take my normal pain meds
But they simply do nothing for me
So I rest most of the day in bed

Wilbur has invited his friend Carl
To join us for dinner this evening
We choose where Nick & Nancy will be
Playing their music with much meaning

I get up and take a shower and dress
I'd really prefer to stay at home
Carl is bringing a new lady friend
I've lost track of how many long ago

The dinner is fine and the music terrific
They are both in exceptional voice
We seldom go out just for dinner
But go where the music is our first choice

So thank you dear God for another day
I know You have not forgotten me
What I really need now is some relief
From this intensive pain I feel

October 24th

Today is Sunday and I could not feel worse
I am crying out loud in pain
My spine and hips feel like they are broken
I don't want to go through this again

I take 6 pain pills throughout the day
But again they have little effect
I then try to relax in a very hot bath
I find the tub too hard for me to sit

I place a towel in the bottom of the tub
Thinking it will soften the blow
It works for a while but then I get out
And towel off and back to bed I go

Wilbur phones Dr. Spiegel at night
And speaks with the Dr. on call
She tells me to take a stronger med.
She is amazed because I am so small

I promise to phone Dr. Spiegel in the morning
Perhaps he can prescribe a new drug
Then I take my sleeping meds
And finally fall asleep like a cat on a rug

I thank God for being with me through this day
It is not at all what I had planned
But I realize that it is not my schedule
And I bow to the power in command

October 25th

I phone Dr. Spiegel at 8:30 sharp
He must have some miracle idea
He is already aware of last night's events
And I am now fully ridden with fear

He tells me that he is very concerned
I seem to be in a downward spiral
I tell him I feel as if I've been shot
In my spine and my hips with a long barrel

The pain has now also spread to my knees
And I barely can walk around my house
I feel like I have truly lost so much
And I look like a little gray mouse

He listens to me and says he is sure
That I do not have a compression fracture
The pain is too global for this to be
And knows we must take immediate action

He prescribes Nuerontin for me to take
It is prescribed exactly for nerve pain
Wilbur heads off to the pharmacy once more
And quickly returns home again

It is hard to pray when you want to die
I cannot go on with this pain
But I pray anyway just to be heard
Please God it is my again

October 26th

Today begins more easily
I get up with much less pain
But that only lasts for a few short hours
And then the pain is back again

I take Bert back to Dr. DeVanney
He is quite certain he has an infection
So he drops off a urine sample again
And Bert feels so much rejection

We head to the carwash to clean my car
I'm thinking of buying a new beetle
We drive to the dealership and talk
And I end up making quite a good deal

I don't want to pick up the car in October
That would put me on the Town's tax list
If I wait until the third of November
I avoid paying taxes until next year's list

Then we head off to the grocery store
To purchase what is on both our lists
We load up the car and finally head
Home for a short rest, what bliss

Bert and Wilbur head off once again
To the pharmacy to pick up Bert's new meds
The doctor has phoned in a new prescription
To deal with Bert's recurring urine infection

Thank you dear God for our blessings this day
Along with the strife and the pain
We know that we are all alive
And we will get to see tomorrow again

October 27th

I begin the day once again in pain
This is really starting to be a drag
I truly want to feel better and better
But that's not what's in today's bag

I will call Doc Spiegel tomorrow morning
And let him know about the pain
He is absolutely the best Doctor on earth
And he will help me just once again

We have a rather quiet day planned
No Doctor or hospital visits to go to
Bert is feeling quite a bit fatigued
And feels his infection is back too

I am very concerned for him today
His spirit is one of defeat
I tell him we cannot give up just yet
He has come so far through this meet

Thank you again God for this day
Although we are racked with pain
We know that You are there for us
And will take care of us once again

October 28th

I rise quite early this morning in pain
And phone Dr. Spiegel at 8:30 sharp
He phones me back in exactly ten minutes
He wants to know exactly what's in my heart

I tell him the pain meds provide some relief
But is too short lived then the pain is back
He tells me to double or triple the dose
Until we can get back on track

I do as he says and find more relief
And follow his instructions to a tee
I can finally move around on my own
And am happy just to be me

I then go and get my hair trimmed
And have a long talk with Doug
He tells me I look very tired indeed
And that's when he gives me a big hug

I finally collapse and cave in for real
And cry on his shoulder for a while
He is always there to comfort me
And I leave with a trim and a smile

I remember to pray especially for him
He has become such a really good friend
He's a young man who has such empathy
I will have my hair done with him until the end

October 29th

Bert's Doctor finally phones today
To verify what we already know
His infection is back and he is in pain
Back to the hospital we must go

Bert has to have another PICC line put in
This is a minor surgical procedure
He then gets his first dose of antibiotic
A new one quite strong we will see

He must go back every thirty-six hours
For a blood draw to measure renal function
For this drug is really quite strong indeed
And could mess up his kidney function

The surgeon finds the same spot in his arm
To implant the new PICC line
Bert feels like a permanent patient
He doesn't even have to wait in line

I put aside my own pain for the day
And extend myself totally to my brother
We return home from the hospital
And he is too tired and sleepy to bother

I tell him he must lie down and rest
If he wants to feel any better
He has been put through enough torture today
And I come upstairs to write a letter

October 30th

We begin the day with another visit
Back to the hospital we go
Bert must have a new blood draw
To see if he gets another dose

His blood count seems to pass the test
So we are sent home this is a big deal
I think my car can drive itself
To the hospital without me at the wheel

Bert is tired and quite worn-out
He retires on the couch again
Now is when my pain really kicks in
I have blocked it out too long once again

I take my meds and lay down for a bit
To try and recover from all that is going on
I pray to our mother and ask for help
Can she see what we've been through all along?

I ask God for an answer to show me a sign
I have not seen it as yet
Perhaps he is talking to me directly
And I am too blind to see it

And so we go on day after day
With hope of a better tomorrow
One without too much pain
Where we can laugh without too much sorrow

October 31st

Today is Halloween for the kids
I remember it as All Hallows Eve
I think of it as a Holy Day
The Eve of All Saints Day I retrieve

I remember going to a special service
And learning about the Saint who was scared
I think it was Saint Ignatius who wore
A mask to hide his face, which he never bared

I keep this day as a Sacred Day
We decide to go visit Granny
It's been too long a time since we've seen
Wilbur's mother a woman so dandy

We drive to her place 1-½ hours away
And have quite a lovely visit
We take her out for a bite to eat
And talk to keep her up on the latest

There is so much to say I never shut up
Wilbur tells me to stop for a breath
But I love her so dearly and can't help myself
There is so much to say at great length

We stay for a while and she is delighted
To finally see us both once again
She asks for Bert who was supposed to come
And we tell her he needs time to rest from the pain

November 1st

Another brand new month begins
A chance to move ahead
I meet with my therapist today
But forget to tell her what's in my head

I have denied my pain for a long time now
In order to focus on my brother
But pain has a way of catching up
And now I must learn to discover

That I must first treat my very own pain
In order to be of any real help
I have been so busy with hospital visits
I forgot to take care of myself

The dream I had the other night
Was about commercial banking at work
It was complicated but I asserted myself
And left not feeling like a jerk

I understand now what a toxic place
The bank was for me to be employed
My boss still calls and tells me how much
He misses my work and my loyalty

November 2nd

Today is my brother's 65th birthday
A day to celebrate indeed
I bake my special lemon cake
And invite the family for pizza

Unfortunately he has 2 Doctor visits
What a way to spend the day
Dr. Oltikar is worried about many things
But especially the infection, which stays

He has been on antibiotics for 4 months
But the infection still returns
He is treated with different antibiotics
None of which can kill the germs

She is seeking an Infection Specialist
Along with a good Oncologist
She is determined to get to the bottom of this
And until then she will not rest

We finally all meet for dinner here
Bert is celebrating his birthday with family
He has not been able to do so for years
As he was always working at the rectory

He opens his presents and is amazed
He tells me we went overboard
I think he is worth every penny spent
He is truly loved and adored

November 3rd

Today is Olivia's 3rd birthday
She is our youngest grandchild
She's a real girly girl with lots of frills
She is certainly not meek or mild

She speaks very well and follows you
And tries to keep up with her sister
Kendra however is 13 years old
But they love each other with kisses

This is also the day I pick up my new car
A brand new VW Beetle Bug
I have been driving a 10 year old Buick
And now I feel as snug in a rug

The car is simply a delight to drive
I feel at home right away
I have driven 2 other beetle bugs
I am very happy for this day

We're off once again to the hospital
For Bert to have his antibiotic treatment
They use the PICC line again this time
The process takes 1 hour to complete

Please bless us this day with good things & hope
We are very much looking to the future
When both of us feel much better indeed
And we can see a bright new picture

November 4th

It is rainy and very cold this morning
With leaves scattered all over the road
We make our daily trip to the hospital
This routine is now getting very old

We stop at the store on our way home
To pick up the few things we need
The barometer has dropped very low
And we are all in a lot of pain indeed

I realize it is Thursday once again
And try to decide about aerobics class
I ponder the warmth of the flannel sheets
But head out the door instead

This is the first time back in weeks
It feels slightly strange to be here
I bring very light weights with me to class
This was the right decision to be clear

I struggle along keeping things low
For I now know not to overdo
Or the price I will pay will be too much
Pain and more pain will be due

I enjoy the stretching at the end of class
It is the best time out of the hour
I come home very tired and weary
And jump into a nice hot shower

November 5th

Bert heads off to the hospital himself
While I go for a hot oil massage
Eileen uses a new pulling technique
And I can feel an electric charge

It is as though while she is pulling
The pain leaves right out of my body
This is the first time I've experienced this
It's as though I'm having a hot toddy

It is wonderful to be free of pain
At least for another few hours
But I find that when I finally return home
I have the sense of smelling springtime flowers

The pain is gone for the rest of the day
This is absolutely amazing to me
I find it hard to believe in fact
That this is how normal people feel

I tackle a few odd jobs around
Which I have not been able to handle
And find such joy in performing them
When I finish I light a candle

I thank God for this day of relief
And hope there are more to come
I don't want to request too much more
And am grateful when the day is done

November 6th

The weekend is here and I can't wait
For our dear friend Joe is coming to visit
I am excited the entire day long
I anticipate and try to remain busy

Wilbur is preparing our dinner tonight
He has even made some dessert
Joe will eat just about anything
He arrives and we introduce him to Bert

He takes the tour of the new foundation
It is too cold for me to join in
Wilbur then takes him out to the barn
His latest project to show him

We have a heavenly visit indeed
Along with a wonderful meal
There is so much to share I catch my breath
I feel like a spinning wheel

Weaving in and out of all the news
There is so much to catch up on
We all enjoy our time together
But soon it's time for Joe to be gone

We make plans to get together soon
And promise to make sure of that
Thank you dear Lord for this joyful day
You always know just where I'm at

November 7th

Another morning at the hospital
I wonder how most folks endure this
Bert is weary and so am I
A free day would seem like bliss

This afternoon we will go to Amy's
To celebrate Olivia's birthday
She turned three years old on the third
We travel the long, long way

The party began very festive and fine
Until the total chaos began
The neighbor directly across the street
Did not like where someone parked their van

Amy was forced to phone the police
And a lengthy battle endured
The neighbor was totally out of control
Which dampened the party for sure

Olivia loved all of her presents
But was not especially well behaved
There was too much commotion going on
Thankfully she stayed inside and played

It was now time to leave the party behind
And we were all glad to just return home
Where things are simple and easy going
Before long Amy was on the phone

November 8th

I awake and remember speaking with Amy
She needed so much attention
I tried my very best to calm her down
But she was filled with rage and vengeance

I told her to put the neighbor's name
In her prayer jar to receive God's blessing
She knew right away this was the thing to do
But she was resistant to learn this lesson

I met with our financial advisor this morning
To roll over the funds in my 401K
I want to be free of the bank entirely
And have a friend whom I know is OK

We trust him implicitly with these matters
He has been helping Wilbur for many years
This represents the final cut with the bank
I am both happy and sad but without tears

He fills out all the paperwork for me
I am not able to write without tremors
He understands this and is very helpful
And he then removes my fears furthermore

The pain has returned just once again
I believe due to all the turmoil in part
Thank you God just the same anyway
You remain very present in my heart

November 9th

This morning it is off to the Oncologist
Who will be meeting Bert for the first time
Dr. Oltikar has made the recommendation
We find her to be very informative and kind

She promises to call a group meeting
With Drs. Oltikar, DeVanney and Whalen
She is true to her word and phones after hours
To report that they have all agreed to a plan

Bert will remain on an oral antibiotic for now
And have one more dose through the PICC line
Which will then be removed hurray, hurray
We'll not miss those visits to the hospital so fine

This is all very good and promising news
Almost too much to take in at one time
As soon as the infection is gone for sure
He'll receive radiation directly to his spine

His PSA levels have dropped to zero
When once they were over forty-eight
The Prostate Cancer is under control
This news is unbelievably great

The traveling to Doctors and hospital visits
Have definitely taken their toll on me
I am tired, weary and not very strong
Please help me God to see

November 10th

We meet this morning at eight o'clock
With Dr. DeVanney once more
Then it is back to the hospital again
For the final treatment to endure

The treatment takes about one hour
And I visit the hospital gift store
I purchase a birthday gift for myself
And then head back to the second floor

Bert is almost finished and then
The PICC line is removed again
We hope he does not require a third
Two is too many and too much pain

We stop at the fabric store to buy more ribbon
For the Christmas presents I have begun to wrap
I realize I will now need more paper as well
But must make another stop before I can nap

We stop at MacDonald's for some lunch
I have a chicken sandwich to eat
Then we head off to the K-Mart store
Where Bert buys Wilbur a Christmas treat

We finally come home so thankful I am
I start the wrapping process again
It doesn't take long before I am tired
And find myself in full-blown pain

November 11th

It is Veterans Day, a time to remember
All those who serve our country
And soldiers who fought in previous wars
To keep us safe from the enemy

Bert & I head off to the pharmacy
And then to the health food store
To purchase the many items we need
Which we find to be many much more

We stop at Alayne's on the way home
And a most pleasant visit we enjoy
Ethan brings out his drawings of cars
And Graham plays the flute to our joy

We then head for home—I am very tired
And want to just slip into bed
But I muster up the courage needed
To go to aerobics class instead

I realize the truth in that old saying
That a little adversity is good for mankind
For kites rise against, not with the wind
How much adversity does God have in mind?

I awake and retire in too much pain
And just try to live each day through it
I find it is getting harder and harder
Please God help me find my way through it

November 12th

I awake again in severe pain
And pray to God for some relief
The pain seems to render me tired
And I'm feeling very lost and weak

I try very hard to understand the pattern
Which seems to elude me somehow
There simply is no pattern to this pain
I must find a way to live with it now

I need to accomplish something useful today
And try wrapping some Christmas presents
The dining room looks like wrapping central
And I wrap until my back is totally spent

Wilbur and I spend some quiet time
After he comes home from his work
I very much need to feel his presence
His job has taken over and I am hurt

I feel like a second rate citizen
Not at all like a marriage partner
We talk for over an hour and one-half
And we both feel a whole lot better

Thank you dear God for the time alone
To speak what is on each others minds
We re-connect through this conversation
And my pain is lessened during this time

November 13th

Tonight is Trivial Pursuit with our friends
We are asked to bring the dessert
I must be the only person left
Who bakes from scratch on this earth

I don't really mind to bring dessert
As I truly and dearly love to bake
I think of my mother as I mix the batter
She is proud and I make no mistake

I bake three loaves of pumpkin gingerbread
And a delicious key lime cake for home
I make a trifle to bring with us
Of the gingerbread, apples and foam

We play the ninety's version of the game
And the men make us look pretty dumb
They win the game by at least a mile
And the women are completely stunned

I'm glad to leave and vow never again
To complain about having a bad hair day
Donna's hair is finally growing in slowly
Judy says she is without a hair astray

She says that she looks like Mr. Clean
And jokes about her being completely bald
I look at her face and notice at once
She has no eyelashes or eyebrows at all

Please bless our friends who are suffering
From the results of chemotherapy
And let them know that they are loved
And that they can find time to be happy

November 14th

I did not sleep very well last night
And got up coughing and wheezing
I went downstairs to take some meds
And went back to bed quite easily

I coughed for a bit longer in bed
And then fell back into a very deep sleep
I guess my body really needed the rest
When I awoke it was quite late indeed

It was well past noon when I finally awoke
Wilbur came up to rub both my arms
One was very sore, as I had slept on it
I felt beat-up and somewhat alarmed

I remember yesterday fainting in the hall
Wilbur caught me before I hit the floor
My blood pressure must be very low
And today I stay entirely indoors

Tomorrow I will see Dr. Spiegel again
I hope I look better than before
He was quite concerned about me
I feel pressure to improve my score

Dear God please help me once again
To accept things that I cannot change
And to deal with the pain more gracefully
And not continue to take the blame

November 15th

I awake much earlier this bright day
I want to finish reading my book
It's about Lance Armstrong and his battles
I finish reading and am totally shook

His life struggles with cancer are shocking
He leaves nothing out in this reading
When I started the book yesterday
I was surprised at the rate I was speeding

The book made me think of life a new way
Never to take anything for granted
For it can be gone in one second flat
Each moment of life must be gently handled

I take Bert with me to see Doc Spiegel
He comes in for a while to chat
But when Bert leaves the tears start to fall
And I feel like a little selfish brat

I tell the Doctor what has been going on
He is amazed at my power and strength
I tell him that he certainly must be on drugs
He tells me of my goodness at length

Thank you God for this great Doctor
He has been treating me for quite a few years
And when he speaks it is with wisdom
He gently erases all of my fears

November 16th

It is Tuesday morning and today we will go
To Manchester to spend most of the day
Bert looks for hours in the choir loft
For music which seems to have flown away

We search a long time and then take a break
Bert plays awhile on the giant pipe organ
His fingers and feet are as nimble as ever
It's as though he never stopped playing

I on the other hand have not sung in years
And must stretch my vocal chords a lot
But I find to my great surprise indeed
That I can sing quite well on the spot

We go to a steak house for I am now hungry
And both order the exact same dinner
It's a fun time for both of us now
Because we are so much thinner

Then it's back to church for choir rehearsal
We sight-read two brand new pieces
I do not find it difficult at all
In fact it seems to come quite easily

Now we leave for home the 53 miles
We talk and listen to the CD player
We choose the best music to listen to
It eases the time we have to travel

November 17th

I awake tired, beat and in great pain
I have over-done things just once again
Good sleep eluded me all last night
In fact I had nightmares that left me drained

Wilbur woke me up at least four times
But I kept falling back into the same dream
Finally he made me wake up fully
It was somewhere around 3 o'clock A.M.

I went back to sleep and got up at eight
To make sure I have baked goodies on hand
I expect the builders to be hard at work
But I look out upon empty land

They ran out of supplies and are not here
I want to go back to the warm comfy bed
But I get up and have some coffee myself
And head into the shower instead

I put on my sweats to be comfortable
Another doctor's appointment is scheduled for two
I lay around the house doing nothing at all
Feeling lousy and also quite blue

I go to my appointment in my sweats
Not normal for me to be sure
But I feel so crummy I do not care
As I pray and leave out the door

November 18th

The doctor told me I had done too much
Oh well, that is no surprise at all
But now I am paying a great big price
I have stumbled and started to fall

Her advice to me is to rest and stay low
This still remains the biggest challenge for me
To lie around, rest and do nothing with my time
Seems sinful and I am left feeling guilty

But I get up and go for my haircut at ten
For me this is always a fun time
We laugh, tell jokes and just fool around
And I never have to stand in line

Doug treats me like a fair-haired princess
As he fusses over me cutting my hair
There is chatter from everyone in the shop
Which is part of the reason I go there

Thank God for Doug and all his staff
They make everyone feel like a star
I certainly needed to see him today
I come home happy and better off by far

November 19th

I awake to the sound of the pounding of nails
The builders are here and the sound is loud
There is so much going on in our lives today
That I say my prayers with my head bowed

They are making such progress it is fun to see
But I am in pain and it's not fun at all
When will this end I want to know?
The answer is never, oh God hear my call

I must focus on Bert for today he will go
To see the Radiation Doctor to get some news
About what they will do and when they will start
We come home quite satisfied for there is good news

The radiation will take fourteen week-days
Just under three weeks in total she says
Dr. Whalen is a genius for her young age
We listen very closely to her wise words of sage

Bert will be finished by Christmas
If they begin at the scheduled time
That would be wonderful for us all
And he will feel better knowing it is behind

We come home from the Dr. and stop on the way
At the bank to switch money around so we can pay
The general contractor who is our friend
Who will see the job through until its end

We have dinner together it is quite good
I thank God for the day and remain in pain
We watch the UCONN women basketball team
They win 107 to 40, wow what a game!

November 20th

I am grateful to awake in much less pain
Yesterday was a bear I could hardly stand
But tonight we are going to dinner and then
To listen to Nick & Nancy our favorite band

Bert is not feeling so good today
I am hoping he'll feel better later on
We want him to join us that is for sure
To celebrate with us is where he belongs

Wilbur is working very hard outside today
Cleaning up the porch getting ready for the cold
He is packing up all the summer furniture
Stacking up the wood to warm his fold

I sometimes think of him as Our Father
Taking care of both me and Bert
He does not mind the task one bit
In fact he takes much pride in his work

I've cleaned up the kitchen and folded the clothes
And that is about all I'm going to do
So I can rest up for this evening out
Without too much fuss or ado

We are celebrating our 8th anniversary
Which is not until Monday next week
But this is the weekend and time to go out
Although the weather is quite cold and bleak

Thank you dear God for this loving man
Who has become my partner for life
I love him so much it is difficult to find words
I am happy simply just to be his wife

November 21st

Last night out was such great fun
The Italia Mia is where we dined
Then headed down to the Ethan Allen
To meet up with our friends and find

To our surprise everyone was there
And then our friend Joe stopped by
To wish us a happy anniversary
We all danced away well into the night

But today I am in the greatest of pain
I must have danced way too much
My hips and spine are throbbing away
I am in need of Wilbur's gentle touch

He massages and rubs away some pain
But it only lasts for a very short time
I wish and pray that this would pass
And that some steady relief I could find

I end up taking my pain medicine
Something that is a last resort
I fight with myself before taking the meds
That's probably why the relief is so short

But I thank God for this pain filled day
At least I am alive and can feel
There are so many others racked with pain
Who must feel that life is unreal

November 22nd

Today is our eighth anniversary
We get up and open our presents
Both of us love what we have received
And are grateful for each other's presence

We have become life partners forever
And we truly feel blessed so dear
For our special love continues to grow
And becomes deeper with each passing year

We feel doubly blessed for we have known
What it is like to live without being loved
We are able to share our innermost truths
Our love is sacred and blessed from above

Bert has gifted us with a gift certificate
For the two of us to go out by ourselves
To have dinner and drinks at Chucks Steakhouse
We can really dress up with glitter and bells

We are so very fortunate indeed
To have Bert living here with us now
For soon his apartment will be completed
I can't wait to make the first entrance and bow

Dear God please continue to bless us all
As we live our lives to the best
Let us remember to thank You always
And to know that we are truly blessed

November 23rd

Today we visit with Dr. DeVanney
To make sure that Bert is OK
It seems that he is doing so much better
We want to be certain it stays

The Doctor issues Bert a good clean bill
It seems the infection is really gone
This is absolutely remarkable
We leave his office with a song

There is no rehearsal scheduled tonight
And so we are not going to Manchester
Instead I will try aerobics class again
And attempt to become stronger and better

The class is quite full when I arrive
This is wonderful for Cindy our instructor
The more people there are in the class
The better for each of us and her

The recreation center wants us to move
To the senior center down the road
This has it pros and cons for all
But we leave it to see what will unfold

Cindy thinks that the gym floor we have
Is the best floor for us to workout
It is gentle and forgiving on the joints
And we don't have safety to worry about

November 24th

It is the day before Thanksgiving
We have so much to be thankful for
Bert's health has made a drastic improvement
Thank God for the changes in store

I awake to the sound of pounding nails
The builders are putting up the rafters
But I find that I am in terrible pain
I want to hear the sound of laughter

I roll out of bed and can barely move
My lower spine feels that something is wrong
It's as if a disk is completely out of place
I go back to bed where I really belong

Heat and massage do nothing at all
To relieve this fierce nagging pain
I take my pain meds without any fuss
And apply a patch of Lidocaine

This freezes the spot for quite some time
But my stomach is feeling quite bad
I almost pass out on the stairway up
And Wilbur puts me back in the bed

I rest for a while and then get back up
This time feeling a slight bit better
The mail arrives and I am again surprised
The handicapped sticker comes with a letter

I do not have to renew the sticker
It is good for the rest of my life
Dr. Spiegel has again come through
And has eased some of my pain and strife

November 25th

It is Thanksgiving Day and what a treat
To say thank you for all of our blessings
There have been so many throughout the year
Along with many new lessons

Each of us has been given a different role
In this ever changing game of life
Just to think of where I was last year
Dealing with pain and wrought with strife

Thinking that work was my only calling
And then that was taken from me
I tried so hard to recover what was lost
It took a very long time for me to see

That God had a different calling for me
I was moved to create these writings
To try to help others deal with chronic pain
And to know God's love is always enlightening

We have our turkey just the three of us
It is the first time Bert is with family
He was always busy with music in church
And now he has a home and a family

Thank you dear God just once again
For letting us see Your everlasting light
And to know that when we surrender ourselves
You can help us to conquer any great fight

November 26th

It is the day after Thanksgiving Day
And we are still counting our many blessings
We have been blessed in so many ways
Lots of turkey and lots of dressing

While many go hungry we eat to excess
This seems so sinful it is bothering
We should all moderate what we eat
And share with those who have nothing

We do our best at this time of good cheer
But what about the rest of the year
Can we make the time to help others?
The seasons of need are there all year

I am in pain but want to do more
I am thankful for we are not in need
The many long days that easily go by
Are precious to me, here is the seed

The seeds of blessings must be shared
With those we do and don't know
I am making a promise to volunteer
When I feel better and am able to do so

November 27th

Bert met with Doug yesterday
And was treated to a hair cut and color
He looks and feels so much better now
He can go out by himself without another

He can drive himself to and fro
To his Doctors or to the store
I am truly most grateful for this
I don't have to go along anymore

Tonight we are driving to Manchester
To an annual Folk Group Party
It will be fun to be with lots of friends
And share some laughs good and hearty

But when we leave I have an attack
Of asthma, I cannot breathe
All the way home I choke and gasp
Whatever is happening to me?

I have not been bothered with asthma
Going on at least five years
But tonight is bad, I think the worst
And cry many, many new tears

I take some meds and it settles down
At least I can get some sleep
I want to get up and have something to drink
But when I try I find I'm too weak

November 28th

Today is Sunday a day of rest
But rest is not for me this day
The asthma continues for a long time
It does not respond to meds so I pray

It finally slows down by afternoon
And I go back to wrapping presents
I am almost through with the process
And realize I've gone over the limits

I want everyone I know to share with me
In the joy of just being alive
I purchase a gift for an unknown child
It feels so good to me inside

Wilbur and Bert take off for a ride
They go to the "Chocolate Belgique"
They come home loaded with goodies
Lots of great chocolate to eat

I delve into one and find it divine
Then I go back for a second
The chocolate is so very rich
It tastes like it must be from heaven

I am still in much pain throughout the day
I thought this would be such a diversion
But I am a fool to think this way
I return to my own prayer version

November 29th

The beginning of another week
Bert must go for x-rays and tattooing
They make permanent spots on his spine
This will identify the exact spot for radiation

He will go to the hospital later this week
For a CAT scan just to make sure
That there are no other problems in sight
And that he might finally be cured

The radiation appointments have all been set
For the same time each and every day
His treatments will last for 14 days
Except for the weekends and holiday

He is anxious a bit so I will go
To hold his hand or to serve if I'm needed
Or just be there sitting patiently outside
Praying for the Doctor and him on my beads

He will be finished on December 28th
Just in time to celebrate the New Year
With many or just a few good friends
To toast to good health with cheer

November 30th

We awake to the sound of builders hammering
It is bright and cold out this day
But the weather does not seem to hamper them
They are happily pounding away

What a nice thing to hear the noise
And watch Bert's new home take shape
We are all anxious for it to be complete
And so for the workers I bake

I try to make them something homemade
For their ten o'clock morning break
They are very appreciative to have
Some hot coffee and something to eat

It's the last day of a very long month
Filled with hospital and Doctor visits
I hope that by the end of the year
There will be fewer and fewer visits

Thank you Dear God for all the time
We have gotten to spend together
Bert's birthday and then our anniversary
Whatever could be better?

December 1st

I awake to the sound of wind and rain
And then promptly fall back to sleep
But the nightmares return and I am afraid
I lay awake and begin to weep

Last week I dreamed that I had drowned
After suffering the asthma attack
But this time the dream rendered me unable
To take care of myself laying flat on my back

I met with the therapist this afternoon
And shared more of my continuing nightmares
She gently explained that they are just feelings
And to try not to be quite so afraid

I cried about the pain in my back
She insisted that I call my bone Doctor again
I promised to do so tomorrow morning
And we talked about the gripping new pain

I told her about my mother's cancer
And that I was truly afraid and scared
She said that not knowing was just as bad
That I should go in fully prepared

Be with me God when I call to You
To schedule the x-rays and whatever else
Dr. Spiegel will respond to my call
I know that praying will certainly help

December 2nd

Today is another trip to the hospital
It is getting to be rather routine
Bert will be having a CAT scan done
And I will be reading a magazine

We are in and out in a very short time
Then come home to have a good rest
So much time has been spent on these trips
But the doctors seem to know what is best

We all have supper together tonight
I'm grateful for the time and repose
I am tired and scared for all of us
I pray for our family and for all those

People, who suffer, we've seen a lot
Spending many days at the Cancer Center
The hospital is building an addition already
To house the new doctors who will enter

It is humbling to be here for any reason
And to see what really goes on
Treatments of all sorts, chemo and such
And of course the important radiation

December 3rd

I've finally finished wrapping the presents
That I have been at for three weeks time
I'm done wrapping, taping and putting on bows
What a feeling, most truly sublime

I started the shopping early in the Fall
Using catalogues calling over the phone
I found some rather unusual gifts this way
And I got to do the shopping at home

No malls or crowds or bustling around
This is the best way to get the job done
I was able to order just the right presents
And to shop for each and everyone

Wilbur is laughing at my early success
The dining room looked like a bomb exploded
But I cleaned it all up and say, "who is next"
To use the space fully cleaned up and loaded?

With paper, tissue, tape, ribbons and tags
All set out very neatly on the table
The men in this house will not take advantage
They will probable use bags and a label

Bert had a meeting with Dr. Brandt today
To receive his first IV Drip of Zometa
This is to help his bones stay strong
While undergoing the next stage of treatment

What a wonderful thing these new cancer drugs
They are given with such ease and devotion
It is hard to imagine working in this place
Without giving in to one's emotions

December 4th

Today is a day I'd prefer not to repeat
My pain is at its highest level yet
I need some relief and I need it now
I feel tortured and think, "is this a test"?

My Fibromyalgia has never been worse
I cannot bear to touch my own skin
I take a hot shower hoping to relax
The water hurts as it bounces off my skin

My entire body is totally involved
In this severe unrelenting pain
Please send a Guardian Angel to me
As I fear this will never end

Wilbur comes up and rubs me with lotion
His touch has me writhing in pain
He continues to rub and when he is through
My legs start to rumble like a fast moving train

He holds my legs as the trembling slows down
I have never felt like this before in my life
My body is shaking uncontrollably
I feel like someone is wielding a knife

The pain starts to ease and I look up in wonder
Just exactly what is happening here?
Wilbur thinks he has just released the energy
That was causing my pain to be so severe

Thank you dear God for my wonderful friend
My husband and my partner for life
I am so blessed to have found him somehow
He's been wonderful throughout this insidious strife

December 5th

I lay in bed awake for quite some time
I must be in someone else's body now
For the body I went to sleep in last night
Is not here and I am wondering how

The pain is not with this body today
Where on earth has it possibly gone to?
I'm afraid to move for fear it will return
Slowly I arise and step on my own shoe

Something very mysterious is happening
Just what it is I am not clear about yet
I'm just beginning to learn about trust
In God I can surely place my bet

He is working with someone else's hands
To deliver the healing power of human touch
How is it that I can have so much love
And at the same time hold it all in so much?

I must learn to be open to other methods
To experience God's love for me
He sends me His love in many different ways
It is my job to learn how and to see

December 6th

The beginning of another new week
Bert must be at the Doctor's by nine
He will receive a shot of Zoladex
To help his recovery which is going fine

Then we will go to the Cancer Center
Where they will draw some more blood
To be sure the Zometa he received last week
Has not caused his kidney levels to flood

He calls this place "Dracula's House"
I am happy not to be wearing his shoes
The trauma to his body has been no less
Than if he were drinking lots of booze

I am still dealing with residual pain
Along with worry and concern for my brother
As if my own pain weren't enough
I'm caught in a whirlwind and feel smothered

We come home to sleep for the rest of the day
There is nowhere else we must be
We all spend a wonderful evening together
And we go upstairs and watch some TV

Thank you again God for helping us along
Just to make it through another day
We know we are on the right path indeed
If we simply stop long enough to pray

December 7th

I awake to snow and freezing rain
Not a pleasant day that is for sure
But I am determined to find a tree
To that end we head out the door

We drive to Southbury 40 minutes away
The tree that I wanted was previously sold
But the store will not release said display tree
Until sometime next Monday I am told

I plead my case with the store manager
She says we must wait until two
Bert goes and gets something to eat
I wait by the platform not moving a shoe

Finally the tree manager arrives on time
He says we can have the floor sample
There is no box to put it in and so
We ride in my VW whose space is not ample

Thank goodness the tree comes in three parts
We look like fools in the parking lot
However are we going to fit the three pieces
Inside my VW bug and not on top?

One part goes in the backseat while another
Fits into the trunk, the third and last piece
Rides in the passenger seat and Bert
Sits uncomfortably in the back to say the least

We arrive home safely somehow by sheer luck
Looking like a car load of trees
But Wilbur comes out to help us unload
Just shaking his head in the breeze

December 8th

Today we meet with our friendly lawyer
For Bert must set up some papers
A Living Will and Appointment of Health Care
To ensure things are in order for much later

We have provided the information earlier
So this takes very little time at all
Then Joe treats us all to lunch
We talk, relax and have a ball

We present Joe with his Christmas present
A book about the history of Law in America
We are pleased to be able to give this gift
He is taken aback by our generosity

We are truly blessed to have Joe in our lives
He has become such a good friend
We worked together for only three years
But we will remain friends to the end

Thank you dear Lord for our blessings this day
And for all You have bestowed upon us
For good friends are life's greatest gifts
We can be free with them and they with us

December 9th

This morning I treat myself to a haircut
And I bring in a gift for Doug
He also has become a very good friend
I always enter and leave with a big hug

Now it is off to the Cancer Center
And Bert's first treatment of radiation
He is scared and troubled as I can tell
I pray as he goes through the motions

I cannot express on paper in words
How much of a friend he has become
We never before spent much time together
And Wilbur and he are also having such fun

We come home and he rests for a while
I am holding in my feelings and pain
I do not dare to share them with him
As his fear is so much greater than

My pain, which seems to soar at times
Especially when difficulties arrive at the door
But we are all learning the meaning of pain
It manifests itself in many ways more

I am trying so hard not to worry so much
And learning that God wants me to pray
For worry is simply a waste of time
That prayer is having faith everyday

December 10th

I wake up reeling in pain again
But I'm having a massage with Eileen
She kneads my skin with soothing oil
And I truly wonder where I've been

All these weeks just writhing in pain
Is a waste of my energy and time
I need to relax much more than I do
And take time to simply rest and recline

Resting is always good therapy
Wilbur reminds me of this every day
What is it I'm so busy doing instead?
That I seldom listen to my heart song play

I am troubled with my eldest daughter
She is having a biopsy done today
She received a bad pap-smear test
I have so many prayers to pray

It's as though God is throwing adversity
And distractions directed my way
I have so many people to pray for
That I forget myself along the way

I do not have time to focus on myself
This is probably a very good thing
When God calls to me on the phone
I am finally ready to listen for the ring

December 11th

Today I am having a MRI done
On my lower lumbar spine and tailbone
This is the source of my greatest pain
I do not want to go through this alone

Wilbur is up taking an early shower
When the hospital calls on the phone
To ask if we can be there at nine o'clock
Instead of 10:30 as originally planned

I agree and then take some meds
To relax me through this process
I am truly claustrophobic and I fear
I may throw up and really make a mess

They get me settled and give me earphones
Partly to quiet the noise of the machine
But I find classical music to listen to
And I lay very still; I'm a little stringbean

The meds do not take and I'm very alert
But I take this time to really pray
What a relief when it is finally over
We come home and I fall asleep right away

Tonight is Trivia at Alice and Bob's
And I'm not feeling very enthused at all
But the time will take my mind away for a while
In the end I'm surprised—we all have a ball

I have brought little gifts for everyone there
They are all sincerely amazed
Wilbur brings in the rocking horse he made
For Jack whose face has become glazed

December 12 [th]

I awake and remember the fun we all had
Last night as we chatted and played
Trivial Pursuit with a wonderful meal
I am so thankful for again I had prayed

That I would feel better by going out
And meeting with friends we truly love
Some good wine to drink and plenty of fun
What wonderful blessings from above

I answered quite a few questions right
I am really quite surprised at that
For things get buried in the back of my head
And I cannot usually call them back

It's a lazy day sitting by the woodstove
Which is taking the chill away
Bert and I work on our Christmas lists
For soon we will be sending greetings your way

I speak with John Scherer on the phone
He lives in Seattle a long distance away
He is so happy to hear my voice and says
He will contact and throw some agents my way

I am so very blessed to know and have him
In our very large circle of friends
He will call me back either later today or
Tomorrow after searching his contacts and friends

December 13th

Bert is meeting with our financial advisor
To discuss his well earned pension
He doesn't want to take it all right now
He wants to leave some for me to spend

This is a very gracious offer from him
I am unable to advise him in any way
Hopefully he'll find exactly the right advice
From a professional early today

Perhaps my results will be into the Dr.
Along with my daughter's as well
We could all use some happy news this week
Good news ringing clear as a bell

It's been a tough haul these past six months
But we are all close family now
So we pull together as best as we can
God will surely lead us somehow

With radiation treatments and DR's appointments
Our schedule has been very full
But in between we find the way
To reassure that we'll all together pull

God has allowed us to see some things
That otherwise we might never have seen
Like it or not we have deep respect
For the professionals whose wit is very keen

December 14th

Today I'm off to see Dr. Spiegel
For a new bone density test
The results are not very good at all
I frown when he tells me the rest

The two years spent on Fosamax
Have had no results for me
In fact I've lost more bone through this
A big problem faces us, what's to be?

He wants me to start a brand new drug
Forteo is the brand name of it
It's self administered by daily injections
I don't like this idea one bit

The rat studies show some bone cancer
This does not thrill me at all
I think of my mother who died of it
But I'm also afraid that I will fall

Bert and I head off to Manchester
To choir practice for the festival
I make it through until the end
That's when my legs begin to fail

The shaking begins uncontrollably
I am unable to walk or move
Thankfully Liz is there to help
She rubs my legs ever so smooth

She draws out the raging energy
That seems in my legs to be stored
This is not the first time I've experienced this
I am terrified and embarrassed for sure

It takes one half hour for me to calm down
I cannot believe this has happened again
I pray to God for some long lasting relief
From this awful continual pain

December 15th

A day of well-needed rest is here
I sleep in until around ten
There is nothing pressing for this day
I am so grateful once again

I get up and begin the Christmas cards
Which have been here since September
Bert has made a computerized list
This is great for I can't seem to remember

The writing goes fairly swiftly for me
I am amazed at how easily this works
I get about halfway through the list
Then my writing arm begins to hurt

I rest for a while and call it a day
As the list is very, very long
I take Bert to his radiation treatment
We stop to buy groceries on the way home

Tonight is Ethan's school concert
He has been playing the trumpet quite grand
In sixth grade he is playing with others
The eighth graders in the advanced band

We happily attend and find to our delight
That he is playing in three bands
The concert, the symphony and the jazz
He is simply amazing and we all clap hands

December 16th

We awake quite early on this morn
The builders are replacing a window
They begin at about a quarter to eight
They are in our bedroom and so

We must vacate our resting-place
That they may continue their work
I get up and mosey around the house
Have some coffee and then back to work

I want to finish the Christmas cards
So that they can finally be mailed at last
I complete the cards quite happily
Writing notes and finishing the list

Then it's off to meet the dietician
For Bert to get some ideas on how
He might deal with the stomach distress
Caused by the radiation, oh wow

So far he has had no reaction at all
He is off all vegetables for now
He is halfway through his treatments
We all hope for the best somehow

We come home and have a relaxing dinner
Of chicken and mushroom delight
Wilbur cooks while we both rest up
For there is nothing to do tonight

I bake a new recipe of chocolate nut bread
To feed the workers for tomorrow's break
They are so happy to be working here
We treat them special, which they think is great

December 17th

A Friday and a very busy day ahead
I am to meet a new Doctor this morning
Dr. Trowbridge is a Physiatrist who deals
In musculoskeletal and neuromuscular workings

I'm quite a bit nervous as the time approaches
But Doc Spiegel would never steer me wrong
The visit goes smoothly and I learn that the pain
Is from a mis-alligned SI joint near my tailbone

He also informs me that I need more vitamins
To keep what is left of my body's small sake
Healthy, strong and able to serve me
And recommends such supplements to take

It is now off again to the Cancer Center
For Bert's daily radiation treatment
After today he'll be halfway finished
With only seven more days left to complete

Now it is time for my therapist visit
A lot of visits to cram into one day
This visit goes well but I am now tired
I want to go home and just pray

But it's off to my daughter's to watch the boys
While Alayne and Brian attend a party
The boys and I have much fun playing games
That we all laugh together good and hearty

They shower and then they head up to bed
I tuck them both in with much love
Ethan has given up his bed for me
I am once again blessed from above

December 18th

When I awake, the family is already up
They are all so busy with chores
Brian is teaching ski instructors while
Alayne is making breakfast for the boys

I have some coffee to warm myself up
Their house is chilly and I'm not warm
Then I head down the road, which takes me
Happily to our warm, cozy home

I have a bite to eat this morning
And then am able to rest for a bit
Before we all head out to Kendra's game
Which they win handily what a hit

Bert has never before seen Kendra play
Basketball, which is her favorite game
I present she and Tanaja with their presents
Pictures of both of them in basketball frames

They are both delighted two very best friends
We have come to love Tanaja dearly
She is always there for Kendra and vice-versa
Their friendship serves them both very clearly

Now it is off to our daughter Amy's house
To celebrate Christmas with gifts and good food
For Kendra will be flying to Florida soon
To visit with her Grandfather and others so good

Everyone is happy with the gifts they receive
We are all thankful for each other
Although I'm quite happy while we are there
I'm also quite glad when this event is over

December 19th

A day of complete rest is just what I need
Wilbur and Bert go out to cut down a tree
I have already put mine up and decorated it
But we usually have not one but two trees

My artificial tree is standing in the living room
All decorated in a Victorian theme
Wilbur's tree must be fresh cut and real
And has a much more eclectic theme

I am happy to stay home to read and write
While they scurry about in the cold
I am still in pain, which I wish would cease
I am headed in the right direction I am told

Doc Spiegel phoned to advise me that
My vitamin D count was a great deal too low
And so he sent in a prescription for me to take
50,000 mgs to take four weeks in a row

So here I sit in front of the computer
Writing these poems for me and you
I truly hope these words help someone else
Who is suffering with pain and feeling blue

A better tomorrow is always at hand
With improvements in body, mind and soul
New drugs appear almost every day now
To help each of us to become whole

December 20th

The beginning of another new week
One of the last ones of this great year
I get up early and have coffee with Wilbur
I'm starting to feel some holiday cheer

I decide to bake some banana nut bread
But change the nuts into chocolate chips
The result is fantastic and we all enjoy
A new recipe that proves to be a hit

The baking bug has gotten to me again
Something that I really like to do
It must come from my Italian heritage
Mother was always baking something new

Now it is time to take my brother Bert
For his radiation treatment just once again
We arrive and everyone is so warm and cheerful
They're a special group of women and men

We come home and find Wilbur lamenting
About the Christmas tree he cut too short
We tell him that we will find another
And to try and be a good sport

Thank you dear God for another day
To spend with my family so dear
Later this week I'll go to Physical Therapy
Something I'm finally beginning not to fear

December 21st

Today begins as usual as most
We get up and have breakfast quite normally
Wilbur goes out to the backyard to find
A very large beautiful Christmas tree

He cuts it down and brings it inside
To dry off and warm up somewhat
Before setting it in the sitting room
Where we will all string lights and decorate

There is the usual grumbling and stress
While trying to get the lights just right
An event where I simply leave the room
A good thing as I avoid risking a fight

I phone my daughter to learn the results
Of the biopsy she had last week
I learn that she has cervical cancer
I get off of the phone and weep

She will have surgery in about two weeks
I desperately want to be there for her
But I'm not sure if I will have enough strength
I will bow down my head in prayer

Surely God would not have lead us this far
To simply leave us all in this much pain
I don't understand but I will try harder
To learn this lesson He has planned

December 22nd

I awake this morning feeling morbid and gross
Remembering my phone call of last night
I am praying just as hard as I am able
That the surgery will turn out all right

Wilbur is still fussing around with the tree
We realize that we're almost out of heating fuel
Neither my brother nor I can take the cold
Wilbur phones for a new tank and a new bill

The new tank will serve the addition as well
As our house which was in need of one
Soon a new furnace will also be installed
With air conditioning and two separate zones

The builders are finishing putting on the roof
So that they can begin the work inside
At least it is not below freezing today
Monday it was 3 degrees cold outside

We gift the workers at their break time
They are delighted with the presents they receive
We wanted to be sure that they were all gifted
Before it became Christmas Eve

They continue their work on the roof
The roof is three-quarters completed now
I cannot wait until the roof is done
Then they can begin the work inside oh wow!

December 23rd

I awake in pain but in a peaceful mind
I take my vitamins and have breakfast
I relax and look at the Christmas Tree
All decorated and completed at last

I think of baking but run out of time
Bert must be at radiation by one
In order that I can be at physical therapy
To correct the damage that has been done

Wilbur takes me to my therapy appointment
He drops me off; runs his errands in flight
I cannot believe the relief that I receive
I even ask if I can spend the night

The process begins with deep muscle massage
Then continues with cortisone ultrasound
They then move on to TENS with moist heat
To relax muscles which were previously bound

I am in awe of the relief I have found
With just one appointment so far
I look forward to next week when I can feel
Relief beyond what I have felt so far

I truly thank God for leading me here
Through my bone doctor who has such wisdom
I am so relaxed I have dinner and wine
And look forward to more treatments to come

December 24th

It is Christmas Eve and I am overwhelmed
By God's grace bestowed upon me
I have heard from all of my truest friends
And am graced by the blessings that be

Tonight we will go to Alayne and Brian's
My daughter and son-in law's home
A lovely evening is planned for us all
I can hardly wait for the time to come

I have chosen the very best gifts for all
Since September I have been shopping
Truly hoping that the presents they receive
Will leave them all happy and hopping

The Christmas Spirit is alive and well
In almost all of the folks that we meet
The providers at the Cancer Center
To the folks that we meet on the street

The evening is here and we all feel good
We are filled with hope and love
To realize what we have all been through
Always blessed by God's grace from above

CHRISTMAS DAY

The day long awaited is finally here
The birth of our Lord in a stable
I am moved to tears as I realize
That my brother has never before been able

To celebrate this day with his family
He has always been playing in church
I am most conscious of the meaning of this day
And feel like the giver, Mother Earth

Wilbur's son Andrew arrives at about eight
We were not expecting him until around ten
Wilbur is making breakfast for all of us
Scrambled eggs, bacon, muffins and then

The smell wafts upstairs and I finally get up
Slowly making my way down the stairs
I greet Andrew with a big Christmas hug
He responds like he truly cares

We all sit down and enjoy our meal
We exchange presents with him
Andrew heads off for the rest of the day
He is eager to leave; it hurts to watch him

We then begin the grand opening feat
My brother is totally overwhelmed
Wilbur is feeling equally the same
In awe of the gifts that abound

The present opening begins at ten
And continues until after four

I am making up for thirty years lost
There's a mountain of paper on the floor!

December 26th

The day after, we are all very tired
I sleep in until well after ten
I awake and find to my delight
Two smiling and contented happy men

Everyone is still in total awe
I broke down in tears last night
My brother is still so very happy
I have never before seen such a sight

He is truly grateful for the last few months
Although he has been through the mill
He is alive and recovering quite well indeed
We have formed a new family; this is Your will

I feel like a fairy princess because
I have been able to give so freely
True happiness for me comes from giving
Not from being the person receiving

Thank you dear God for allowing me
To be the person that You have chosen
To provide some relief from pain and strife
I know first hand about being afraid and frozen

Your words to us are so simple and true
We just need to open our eyes and ears
For You are always near to us
Calming us and releasing our fears

December 27th

I awake in great pain just once again
And call for physical therapy
I get an appointment to go at eleven
I drive myself there feeling happy

Knowing that I will get some relief
From this pain in my back and hip
It has been gnawing at me for days
So I gladly and eagerly make the trip

A new therapist greets me this time
She does a good thorough evaluation
She manipulates by body in such a way
I hear things popping when she is done

Now it is time for the TENS Machine
I want to stay here all day long
But I must leave and head off for home
For that is where I really belong

I'm supposed to be at Amy's house
Caring for her after her hospital stay
But the relief I find is too short-lived
Back to bed with pain meds I stray

I feel like a failure and a good one at that
But I must take care of myself first
This is a big disappointment for all of us
As I move myself to the top of the list

This is the very first and strange time for me
That I've not been there for someone else's need
I ponder this for a short while and know
God is always there to take the lead

December 28th

Today is Bert's last radiation treatment
It is almost a real celebration
Wilbur picks up his daughter Cory
While I take Bert in for treatment by ten

We have a blueberry pancake breakfast together
Which proves to be a real treat for us all
For Cory lives in Salt Lake City
And when she visits we always have a ball

Wilbur seems a bit nervous today
He wants everything to be just right
Why can't he let go and let God lead the way?
He is snippy and a bit uptight

He still has a contest with his former wife
Of who can outdo each other
When Cory visits she splits her time with us
But cannot do so this time because of my brother

We take her out to visit with family
Bert does not feel well and stays home
Wilbur and I are touchy with each other
Like two dogs fighting over the same bone

We talk about this when we drop her off
And then Wilbur heads upstairs to bed
I stay up reading and writing
And praying weak prayers instead

It is hard to pray when you're angry and sick
I ask God for the courage to stay
Please help me to relax and learn from this
I know You will not lead me astray

December 29th

Today I will have physical therapy again
My sacroiliac joint is "out of joint"
Who would have thought that being so flexible
Would get me in trouble to this point?

Hyper-mobility might be good for gymnasts
But not for a woman with brittle bones
The choices are becoming more limited
As I travel along this journey toward home

I have learned many things throughout this year
Some of the lessons being too close to home
I see friends who have lost all of their hair
Lost to chemo when things have gone all wrong

I'll never again have a "bad hair day"
Or complain about my pain out loud
For what I have seen at the Cancer Center
Is enough to keep my head bowed

"It is not the years in your life that matter
Rather it is the life in your years"
My favorite quote comes from Abe Lincoln
And has many times brought me to tears

And so as this book nears its end
I hope that you might have found
That trusting in God is the only way
To keep well with both feet on the ground

December 30th

Today I celebrate the day of my birth
I quietly give thanks to my mother
To have such love to give to me
And to my very dear brother

It was my custom when mother was alive
To send her red roses on my birthday
Since she has passed on I keep the tradition
Selecting a special person to honor on this day

This year I have chosen Debbie Sanford
One of the best mothers I have ever known
She cares for her children and others as well
Some coming to know her as their own

Tonight we will all go out to dinner
And I expect to receive a toast
But a child's birthday is really about
The parents who gave up the most

And so I will pray for all mothers today
Along with all mothers to be
I may not have had everything as a child
But today I am happy just to be me!

December 31st

The very last day of the year is here
A year filled with tears of sorrow and joy
As I reflect on each memorable event
I continue to be filled with wonder and awe

We've each lived through some very rough spots
Wondering if we would make it through
When you give it your best and trust in God
There is simply nothing that you cannot do

We've lived through cancer and chronic disease
And grew stronger each step of the way
We rejoice not because everyone is cured
But because of the path we have stayed

It is difficult to let go and let God take over
But always find that when we finally do
Everything all at once becomes easier
Our job is merely to see it through

There will always remain decisions to make
We pray for wisdom and healing each day
God does not make us do anything
He guides us along as we pray

My wish and prayer is that love will rule
And that bitterness will soon pass away
That the New Year will bring more happiness
To each of you day after day!

Happy New Year

About the Author

Lois began writing poetry & music at age 11. She has composed many pieces of music for piano and guitar. With the onset of disability, Lois decided to focus on her time and talents providing readers with a journey of embracing life while living with chronic pain. Lois resides with her husband Wilbur and her brother Bert in a fully restored 1820 farmhouse in CT, along with their collective cats: Ella, Sarah & Miss Mary.

0-595-34705-3

Printed in the United States
27547LVS00002BA/1-33

9 780595 347056